THROUGH THE YEAR WITH BRIAN D'ARCY

Brian D'Arcy CP

Through the Year
with Brian D'Arcy

the columba press

First published in 2008 by
the columba press
55A Spruce Avenue, Stillorgan Industrial Park,
Blackrock, Co Dublin

Cover by Bill Bolger
Origination by The Columba Press
Printed in Ireland by Betaprint, Dublin

ISBN 978-1-85607-623-4

1 January

Here's my way of wishing each and every one of you a happy, healthy and prosperous New Year:

In January, the month of darkness and frost. Be with us, Lord.

In February, the month of rain, wind and snow. Be with us, Lord.

In March, the month of farmers, lambs and new life. Be with us, Lord.

In April, the month of swallows, growth and green grass. Be with us, Lord.

In May, the month of the cuckoo, the flowers and summer. Be with us, Lord.

In June, the month of examinations, the mid-summer and sun. Be with us, Lord.

In July, the month of holidays, the dry grass and summer end. Be with us, Lord.

In August, the month of harvest, wheat and corn. Be with us, Lord.

In September, the month of fruits and schools. Be with us, Lord.

In October, the month of falling leaves, nuts and Halloween. Be with us, Lord.

In November, the month of darkness and emptiness. Be with us, Lord.

In December, the month of the gift, the light and Our Saviour. Be with us, Lord.

(From *A Little Bit of Life* by Fr Brian D'Arcy)

2 January

Christy Kenneally is a master storyteller. There are times when he is as daft as Spike Milligan, then again he can be as profound as St John of the Cross.

Even old jokes come alive in Christy's imagination.

'Dad, is it true we all come from dust?'

''Tis boy.'

'And we'll all go back to dust?'

'We will boy, why?'

'There's someone coming or going under my bed.'

Small Wonders by Christy Kenneally, Mercier Press, is a delight to read in these busy depressing times.

3 January

New Year is a good time for checking out on life. For me that means checking out how religion helps us cope with the joys and sorrows of life. You don't often see it put like that. Religion has no other useful purpose than to direct us to a compassionate God. For Christianity it shouldn't be a problem, because Jesus is compassion personified.

Christianity's biggest obstacle, though, is the behaviour of Christians.

4 January

Here is a quote from one Gerard Baker, writing in *The Times*. He wrote it because a priest had been good to his father-in-law in his last days:

> 'We have heard a lot about priests in the past year or two. Men whose behaviour has destroyed the lives and tortured the souls of so many innocent people. It sometimes seems as though the very notion of the priesthood has become an object of derision, a suitable subject for scorn ... But from time to time I think it necessary to remind the world that there are other priests out there who will never make headlines, never find themselves the subject of a film, never rise above the level of simple obscurity to the masses, but whose daily willingness to sacrifice their whole lives marks them out as genuinely extraordinary. Not because they are exceptions, but because they are the rule. Perhaps we can occasionally acknowledge – anonymously – those priests who through simple devotion succeed in the quite remarkable challenge of remaking millions of broken lives every day.'

5 January

Saint Charles of Mount Argus
From 3 June 2007 Fr Charles of Mount Argus, this ordinary saint for ordinary people who referred to himself as 'Poor old Charlie,' will be called St Charles of Mount Argus.

He was born in Munstergeleen in Holland on 11 December 1821. He came to Ireland on the feast of Our Lady of Hope, 9 July 1857.

He was a young man who found passing exams difficult. As a teenager he joined the Military Service in the 1840s and even though he was not a success as a solider, it was there he first heard of the Passionists in Belgium and decided to join them when he left the army. He was ordained in 1850 and two years later he was sent to England which was his first contact with the Irish. It was just after the Famine and Irish emigrants were everywhere. He died on 5 January 1893. That date is now the feastday of this likeable, ordinary saint.

6 January

In his book, *All The Pope's Men*, John L. Allen points out that the Vatican is not on top of the sexual abuse scandals at all. It seems more concerned with protecting the rights of the priest and of due process, than it is with protecting the children or their families. It's legalistic rather than pastoral in its approach. There will be big trouble ahead in America and Europe when, according to Canon Law, the church will order bishops to reassign some of these priests to ministry. The book is a must for those of us who thought we knew how the Vatican works but now realise that many men of goodwill can still maintain a system that is often harmful, un-spiritual and a hindrance to spreading the gospel.
(*All The Pope's Men; The Inside Story Of How The Vatican Really Thinks*, by John L Allen Jnr, Doubleday.)

7 January

In his book, *All The Pope's Men*, John L. Allen dispels myth after myth about the Curia.

- It is not a monolithic group who speak with one voice.
- There are many in the Curia who would like to see the birth control decision at least reviewed and probably reversed.
- Some in the Curia favour a greater de-centralisation of power.
- Most surprisingly of all to me was that Cardinal Ratzinger and Walter Kasper disagree on their theology of the church.
- Archbishop Marini, who is the Pope's Master of Ceremonies, often disagrees with, and even ignores Cardinal Estevez who has spent his life trying to reform the liturgy in not very helpful ways.
- From Allen's book it is not clear if anybody is in charge of the Vatican. The offices and commissions are independent of one another. The Pope seems to listen to them, agree with them when it suits him and make up his own mind when it doesn't.
- The Vatican is a political minefield and is hopeless at keeping secrets.
- It is not wealthy. Its endowment is smaller than that of the Catholic University of Notre Dame.

There are huge numbers of people working in the Vatican, most of them priests and bishops who are openly careerists, yet Allen also points out that he met many members who were free of any ambition.

8 January

In any area where 1,000 adults are living, (that probably means about 300 houses and a block of flats), it is likely that:

2 will be blind; 13 will drink to excess and may be alcoholics; 170 will be old age pensioners; 30 will have accidents in the home; 7 will be in a road accident, and every sixth year one will die as a result; 600 will go away for their holidays but 400 will stay at home; 100 will be receiving supplementary benefits; 2 will die of cancer; 20 will be convicted in courts (mostly for driving offences); 100 will be hard of hearing; 20 will need a hearing aid and one will be profoundly deaf. Put another way, this suggests that within a few hundred yards of where you are living, there are many people who need help. So go and do it!

9 January

How does the Catholic Church treat gay people? With compassion? Hope? Encouragement? Read what this gay man has to say and draw your own conclusions:

'The common public perception is that the Catholic Church is completely against homosexual activity and homosexuals themselves. It was only when I picked up the *Catechism of the Catholic Church* that I realised that homosexuals are indeed accepted and that it is only homosexual activity that is looked down upon.

Homosexuals are completely omitted from prayer at Mass. I have never witnessed a prayer for homosexuals and have never heard a priest, yourself excepted, encourage the fair treatment of homosexuals.'

10 January

When a disaster strikes a single country, or a city, grief and death can be understood even though it is still devastating. But on the day after Christmas 2004 we witnessed a tsunami and catalogue of woe that hasn't been experienced on a universal scale, since World War II.

Yet there is a good side to tragedy. In the face of disaster we respond magnificently. The woman in Belfast who turned back from buying a coat in a Sale to give the money to the Asian Disaster Appeal because, 'the coat would only hang in my wardrobe', shows that we are still clothed in ordinary human decency. The way people responded to collections for the fund, the efforts people made, the respect given to the dead and to the living, was truly inspiring.

The bottom line is that there is only one face to grief: no matter how many languages or skin colours suffered, all human hearts break, all human eyes cry bitter tears, all good people respond heroically.

11 January

Everything I need to know about life I learned from a jigsaw puzzle:
Don't force a fit. If something is meant to be, it will come together
naturally.
When things aren't going so well, take a break. Everything will look
different when you return.
Be sure to look at the big picture. Getting hung up on the little
pieces only leads to frustration.
Perseverance pays off. Every important puzzle went together bit by
bit, piece by piece.
When one spot stops working, move to another. But be sure to
come back later (*see above*).
The creator of the puzzle gave you the picture as a guidebook.
Variety is the spice of life. It's the different colours and patterns that
make the puzzle interesting.
Establish the border first. Boundaries give a sense of security and
order.
Don't be afraid to try different combinations. Some matches are
surprising.
Take time to celebrate your successes (even little ones).
Anything worth doing takes time and effort. A great puzzle can't be
rushed.
(Author Unknown)

12 January

Jesus was at pains to point out that all genuine people are welcome
in his community. He invited all people of goodwill to communion.
He would not refuse communion to those who struggle with imperfection. He would not reject those in loving relationships. He
would not humiliate anyone looking for his help.
No matter how tired we've become, we cannot allow heartless
tyrants to high-jack either our loving God or our beloved church.
We have to stand against those who make God ridiculous and irrelevant. We must do it for God's sake.

13 January

Every week I get letters from women who are violently abused by their husbands. Increasingly, though, men write to tell of the mental and physical abuse they're suffering at the hands of their wives. The organisation which helps men is called AMEN.

The Department of Health published a report in 2004 which showed that both partners used violent acts in half of all cases, with the remainder divided equally between male only violence and female only violence.

It's devastating when there is violence in a relationship. Nobody, man or woman, deserves to be brutalised in such a way. Physical violence is destructive, yet it is much more difficult to quantify the damage done by mental cruelty. Children suffer too because, all too frequently, they follow the same pattern in their own lives later on.

14 January

There are people in the church who still have, 'a beneficial influence' in the world. They are to be found in groups of laity who are alive and active and working, sometimes in Parish Groups, but more commonly in secular organisations, Third World Help Groups, teachers, hospitals, but rarely in churches.

I am struggling to find a hopeful trend and that's the only one I can come up with. The laity still have a voice if we tired old clerics would give them encouragement and responsibility. Change will happen anyway, with or without our permission. There's where the real hope is.

15 January

I have no idea if the church as we know it will survive the next twenty years, never mind the next century. That's why I've a sneaking regard for Jim Wallis who is predicting the shape of the church during the next hundred years.

Some of his predictions are coming true right now. Two years ago there was an open hostility to religion. But now there's evidence of a meeting of minds. The ultra conservatives are beginning to realise that we must care about poor people more than we care about doctrine. On the other hand, the out and out liberals are coming to the realisation that you do need principles, standards and laws if society is to survive.

I hope Wallis is right when he says that women will blossom into leadership roles within the church. At present I can't share his optimism though I do share his enthusiasm.

16 January

I don't know about you, but the most effective ad I have seen in a decade or more was the one made by *Make Poverty History*. Do you remember the 'clicks' featuring celebrities like Brad Pitt, Kate Moss and Kylie Minogue? It had the unforgettable punch line, 'One child dies every 3 seconds.'

But can you believe this? The most effective ad on television has been banned. The media regulator ruled that the 'click' adverts were a political message and therefore fell foul of the law.

If an advert as effective as 'click' is against the law, then it's time the law was changed.

17 January

The last meeting I had with Johnny Cash I had the honour of introducing him on stage. As always when he came to Ireland, I got to as many of his gigs as I could. I always knew I was in the presence of a legend, a vulnerable man whom I might never see again.

He told me once that he gave his life to God at the age of 12. He said, 'Whenever I hand it over to him I have an inner peace that only he can give. When I try to run it myself I end up in a complete mess.'

The last time we met he brought his wife June and her two sisters into a small room to ask God's blessing on the show they were about to do. I always remember his final prayer. 'God give me the strength to remember my weakness.' That's how I like to remember him.

18 January

I found the controversy about the priest in Galway who had a child with his partner somewhat confusing. On the one hand it was front page news and the lead topic on numerous talk shows throughout the country. I know it's news, particularly in the local area, but national headline news in this day and age? I don't think so.

I was also impressed by the Pastoral Council in his parish who said that given time they would come to terms with the situation, would try to be non-judgemental, and would have compassion both for the partner and priest. That's a mature attitude to have and it shows how far the laity has come in this country.

And I hope the priest, his partner and their baby are healthy, happy and at peace.

19 January

The Bee Gees used to have a hit song called *Words*. In it was the famous line, 'It's only words and words is all I have to take your heart away.'

Words are our primary way of communicating. They are powerful tools for good or for bad. William Ward once said, 'Our words can cut or comfort, hinder or help, harass or heal, injure or inspire … each time we speak we deliver our own state of the heart address.'

Encouraging words give us a lift.

On the other hand, verbal abuse kills the spirit. Words spoken in anger, guilt or resentment cut to the quick. There was a song here in Ireland with the philosophical title, 'Whatever you say, say nothing.' And if words don't build up and encourage, it surely is better to say nothing.

20 January

Many of the church's problems today arise because of a flawed theology of sexuality. It's the big question nobody wants to tackle. Think of the areas where people find themselves at odds with the church. First is family planning. Second is sex within and outside of marriage. Thirdly, who can go to Communion when they are in a second relationship? How many needless problems have those three issues caused?

I am not saying married priests will solve every problem in the church. But I do say that a married clergy would be a wonderful gift to the church, bringing healthy attitudes about life and sexuality to a dysfunctional all-male clerical club.

I am convinced that had priests and bishops been married, they wouldn't have needed 20 years to come to the conclusion that it was wrong to abuse a child!

21 January

One in six children is severely hungry;
one in seven has no healthcare at all;
one in five has no safe water and
one in three has no toilet sanitation facilities at home.
Over 640 million children live in dwellings with mud floors
or extreme overcrowding.
Over 120 million children are shut out of primary schools,
the majority of them girls.
180 million children work in the worst forms of child labour.
1.2 million children are trafficked each year.
2 million children, mostly girls, are exploited in the sex industry.
Nearly half of the 3.6 million people killed in conflict during
the 1990s (45%) were children.

22 January

If everyone were holy and handsome with 'Another Christ' shining in neon lighting from them, it would be easy to see Christ in everyone. If Mary had appeared in Bethlehem clothed, as St John described, with the sun, a crown of twelve stars on her head and the moon under her feet, then people would have willingly made room for her. But this was not God's way, nor Christ's way, for he is disguised under every type of humanity that treads the earth.
(Dorothy Day)

23 January

Things You Can Learn from a Dog
Allow the experience of fresh air and the wind in your face to be
    pure ecstasy.
When loved ones come home, always run to greet them.
When it's in your best interest, practise obedience.
Let others know when they've invaded your territory.
Take naps and stretch before rising.
Run, romp and play daily.
Eat with gusto and enthusiasm.
Be loyal.
Never pretend to be something you're not.
If what you want lies buried, dig until you find it.
When someone is having a bad day, be silent, sit close by, nuzzle
    them gently.
Thrive on attention and let people touch you.
Avoid biting when a simple growl will do.
On hot days, drink lots of water and lie under a shady tree.
When you're happy, dance around and wag your entire body.
No matter how often you're scolded, don't buy into guilt and
    pout ... run right back and make friends.
Bond with your pack.
Delight in the simple joy of a long walk.

24 January

Martin Luther King said: 'We are supposed to be Good Samaritans
helping the afflicted on the road to Jericho, but it is even more important to make sure that the road to Jericho is transformed so that
men and women will not be constantly robbed as they make their
journey on life's highway.'

'True compassion is more than flinging a coin to a beggar. True
compassion sees that the edifice which produces beggars is restruct-
ured!'

True Prophets make us uncomfortable. And Martin Luther
King was a prophet who pulled no punches. That is why he was
assassinated.

25 January

Football was in the news last weekend. Everybody was talking and writing about David Beckham. David was once a talented footballer, who discovered that he could make more money being a celebrity. Alex Ferguson was the first to try sort him out. Real Madrid were foolish enough to pay mega money for him. They can't complain because they made their profits from him, not on a football field but by selling shirts. So when they claim the moral high ground now it's pathetic.

If David Beckham gets more money from America for not playing football, well why blame him? But who is using whom? If you ask me, David Beckham is playing the media at our own game. And all of us are doing exactly what he wants. David Beckham is getting his money. American football and whoever the other hangers on prove to be, are getting their publicity. Real Madrid got their shirts into places they never would have got them before. Posh has got the house and climate she always wanted.

26 January

David Ervine was a man I came to admire over the years. Given both our backgrounds in Northern Ireland, we each had a long journey to make if we were to meet in the middle.

Often, after our Friday night television shows, we went to the Club where he held forth on his favourite topics – socialism, the failure of the Christian religions to give a voice to the deprived people in their ghettos, and how a distorted history had destroyed the legitimate struggles of both communities here. With his pipe and his pint he was always open about the events that led him into the Loyalist Paramilitary campaign and his disgust for the Unionist leaders who talked up a storm but then deserted their followers when they ended up in jail.

David Ervine was a good man who made the long journey from terrorism to pacificism, long before it was either fashionable or profitable. I always enjoyed meeting him and learned much from him. His wisdom and leadership will be sadly missed in the world of Northern politics.

27 January

'When I stand before God at the end of my life, I would hope that I would not have a single bit of talent left and could say, I used everything you gave me.' So said Erma Bombeck, the housewife- turned-columnist, who spent the last 32 years of her life helping us laugh at ourselves and the everyday routines of family life.

'Too old for a paper round and too young for social security,' she started to write with such engaging humour that her columns quickly syndicated to 700 newspapers, and her books, like *The Grass is Always Greener over the Septic Tank*, became instant best sellers.

After she found out she was dying of cancer, Erma wrote: 'If I had my life to live over, I would have invited friends over to dinner even if the carpet was stained, or the sofa faded. But mostly, given another shot at life, I would seize every minute ... look at it and really see it ... live it and never give it back.'

28 January

'O Lord, help us never to move into stone houses.'

People in the township lived in rows of poorly constructed tin houses. They were hammered together in groups so that it wasn't clear where one family ended and the next family began. The conditions were poor yet each family became part of an even bigger family. Everybody shared too. In those conditions there is no mine and thine, but only ours.

In the well-off parts of the township, stone houses were built and very quickly doors were put on the houses and locks put on the doors. That's when the world of mine and thine began.

Perhaps the reason we in the West are so possessive is because the only world we know is the world of stone houses. There's nothing we can do about it – we are not going to live in communal hen-houses again – but we must also realise that the world of stone houses soon produces rooms with doors and doors with locks and not only does one family not share with the next family, members of the same family don't even share. Unlike some of our friends in Africa, we have every material possession, so much so that the possessions now possess us.

29 January

In 1967, just a year before his assassination, Martin Luther King gave a sermon at Riverside Church in New York which highlighted the good and bad of the American way of life. He quoted John F. Kennedy: 'Those who make peaceful revolution impossible, will make violent revolution inevitable.' We won't give up our comfortable way of life and therefore we snuff out any attempt by the poor in the Third World to get justice.

King went on: 'America must rapidly begin the shift from a thing-orientated society to a person-orientated society. When machines and computers are considered more important than people, then we will never conquer the giant triplets of racism, materialism and militarism.' He was speaking about American society but it makes us all uncomfortable and that is why we rarely hear the speech.

30 January

It's interesting to realise that just as we in Ireland seem hell-bent on the destruction of the family, Britain is rediscovering an ancient truth – namely that families are the building blocks of society. For more than 12 months, Ian Duncan Smith's Social Justice Policy Group examined how crime and deprivation have blighted society. Drugs, alcoholism, debt, illiteracy, hopelessness, crime and the collapse of local communities mean that only a small percentage of children have any experience of the stable family life.

Duncan Smith argues that none of these issues can be properly understood until the collapse of the family is fully examined. It's not so much that there has been a rise in divorce rates, which in fact have remained quite stable over the last decade or so, but the real problem is the high rate of break-up among co-habiting couples. More than half of co-habiting couples break-up before children reach the age five.

Would it be too much to ask our politicians in Ireland, North and South, to learn from the experiences in Britain? Liberal drug laws, extending hours of drinking, giving tax-breaks to co-habiting couples, and a reluctance to do anything to protect marriages, can only have one result – the collapse of society.

31 January

A famous Italian poet Pier Giorgio Welby, who suffered for many years from Muscular Dystrophy, wrote a letter to the President of Italy asking to be allowed to die. Welby was a long time advocate for euthanasia. In his letter he explained to the President that he had battled for 40 years with Muscular Dystrophy and for the last nine years had been attached to a ventilator. He was now losing his capacity to speak, and he finished his letter with this remarkable statement: 'What is left of me is no longer a life. It is an unbearable torture.'

His request for the ventilator to be removed was denounced as suicide. But a doctor defied the law and turned off the ventilator. The diocese of Rome then denied Welby a Catholic funeral.

I was reminded of the very brave decision by the late Pope John Paul II, who in his last days quite rightly refused to go back to Gemelli Hospital because he knew that his breathing would be assisted by a respirator and his food would be supplied through a tube. Rather than go through all that intrusive treatment, Pope John Paul simply said, 'Let me go to the house of the Father.'

For me Welby's decision is in the same category. After nine years on a respirator, he was quite entitled to recognise that his treatment was going nowhere. His request was not for suicide but for an end to an unbearable torture without a future.

1 February

Looking around, a normal priest is aware that a large proportion of his parish doesn't attend church regularly. They come for baptisms, weddings and funerals. They don't need the church at other times. He knows he's irrelevant to their lives – most of the time anyway. They haven't lost faith in God; they have just given up on the church as they experience it.

The young see him as a relic from the past. It's not that they are switched off by the church; it's more that they were never switched on. So much for Catholic schools with their so-called Catholic ethos.

He knows that married couples make up their own minds about sexual morality. They plan their families themselves as effectively as they can and he knows they are right, but dare not say so. There'll be no dialogue, no discussion, just silence. It's a good example of common sense from the people and communal denial by the church.

From the church's position, a most unhealthy state of affairs.

2 February

Last Sunday I looked at pictures taken at soccer matches across England. The number of spectators caught in praying positions was fascinating. There were managers, players and fans with their eyes cast towards the heavens. Others had their eyes closed in deep contemplation. Still others had their hands joined as their favourite player lined up to take a penalty. Half of them were praying he'd score and the other half were praying that he'd miss. Clearly both God and referees have an impossible task.

3 February

Most sensible priests still try to involve every section of the community, but recognise that women are more disillusioned than priests are. Women's ordination cannot even be discussed, and anyway it's taken for granted that women have no rights, but if they ask celibate men nicely, they may be given some 'privileges'. Actually all lay people tell me they have similar experiences.

When he speaks with other priests, he finds two distinct trends. One group, usually the very old and the few young, see no problem. Their way of coping is to deny the problem exists. He understands the old men because they'll hang on for a few years and die peacefully.

The young baffle him because he can't understand why they became priests in today's climate and how they came out of training with such blinkered, intransigent views. Even in his day he was taught that faith is not a static condition but a way of being on pilgrimage. Ideals have to be proclaimed, but can never be made requirements for sacraments. It's common sense and good pastoral care.

4 February

When David Beckham began to wear Rosary beads around his neck, tens of thousands of young people who didn't know what Rosary beads were, wore them as a fashion symbol. Recently, in a class of 30 who were asked who their favourite role model was, 18 said David Beckham and only one said Jesus.

In England soccer clubs are carrying out more and more functions that used to be held in church. All of the big clubs now provide a place where people can be married, have a reception and have photographs taken on their grounds. It's a good business.

A growing number of fans requests that their ashes be scattered on their favourite ground. Birmingham City offer club themed funerals. They can have a blue and white coffin (club colours) and a wake held at the club. They also have a special place where ashes can be interred. Charlton Athletic had so many requests for ashes to be scattered on the pitch that they have created a Garden of Remembrance where already 50 people are buried. Arsenal's new ground will also provide a resting place for their fans.

It's amazing how big business can see how commercial religion is, while most religions bury their heads in the sand and simply give up.

5 February

I was delighted to get a lovely letter from a person who had some good things to say about the priesthood. 'On reading your article on good priests, I just had to write to you. I agree there are many good priests out there but we don't hear about their good work. Last year my mother was diagnosed with cancer, her time was short. Thankfully we could nurse her at home and so the priests began calling when they heard about her illness. There was a parish priest, a young curate and a semi-retired priest in his 80s. Each one came, chatted with my mother, prayed with her and were so good to her throughout her sickness.

My mother died on a Sunday night and the young priest called early in the day and again that evening, realising my mother's time was short. My mother died at 10.30 and he arrived back at 11.15, said prayers with us, had tea and was a great comfort to us. The next morning he was back again and gave us all the support he could.

As long as I live I will never forget the kindness of these priests at such a sad time in our lives. We don't read about these good men but if they were stepping out of line it would be splashed all over the papers.'

6 February

Perhaps rather than condemning football as the new religion, we should learn something from it. If you don't believe 50,000 people can have a prayerful experience together, then you have never been to a football match where your team has won in the last second, thanks to your prayers. I know – I was that soldier.

The biggest lesson that religion can bring to football though is that we don't have a right to success. Sometimes things work out for us, and sometimes they don't. In life and in sport we learn that both are necessary. Fame and fun pass but God is there on the way down to pick us up, which is more than can be said for most football teams. And another thing. A day out at a football match now costs a family about £100 stg. You can spend an hour in church for a lot less than that.

7 February

I was enthused by an essay on leadership which I read recently. The writer compared leadership to a three-legged stool. Three-legged stools never rock. Vital if you are trying to squeeze milk from a reluctant cow.

Good leadership too is dependent on three legs or sources.

The first leg starts with the desire to be a leader, and examines the gifts, talents, drive and interest we have. Have we a passion, an imagination and a vision that won't go away? In religious terms we might call it a vocation. In secular terms it is: Are you suited to the job?

The second source of authority is from above. Who authorises me to be a leader? Who employs me? What manager gave me the job? Have I the authority from the institution?

The third source is from below. Those who are to be led must be willing to be led. They have to agree not to undermine the authority of the leader. If we want to be led we must sacrifice some of our own self interest and this becomes easier if the leader inspires confidence.

The difficulty is that some leaders have only one source of authority, and collapse immediately. Others can get by with apparent effectiveness on two sources of leadership. But it won't last either.

8 February

'Estimates put the number of children orphaned by AIDS in Africa at over 11 million. This has a devastating effect on children. But the wider community is also badly effected because AIDS tends to take out people at an age when they should be at their most productive.

The United States is to spend $15 billion on tackling the HIV/AIDS crisis in Africa and the Caribbean over the next five years.

According to UNICEF new infections of HIV occur at 6,000 a day, or 4 every minute, more than half of them in people between 15 and 24 years old.

For it to be effective, the main thrust of the anti-AIDS drive must therefore be directed at prevention and education programmes among young people.'
(GOAL)

9 February

Bullying is a major problem in Irish schools, homes and work places. It is also, in my opinion, the root cause of many suicides in our country. Because of the nature of suicide, it's hard to prove a direct link with bullying. However, the results of bullying are fear, anger, sadness, humiliation, the dismantling of self-belief. Those are the circumstances that will drive a person to think of suicide.

In modern Ireland bullying is almost institutionalised. In our efforts to be top of the league of greed, we are willing to sell our soul. If this means bullying our way to the top, then so be it.

Experts tell us that bullies intimidate others mentally, physically and emotionally. It means putting others in uncomfortable situations, personal intimidation and intentionally hurting the weak. You can see it in physical aggression, extortion, abusive behaviour, deliberately excluding others, slagging them off, name calling, hitting people, making cutting remarks, spreading rumours, true or false, about others. They are all bullying and hurtful in their own way.

10 February

Zaki Badawi was the head of the Muslims in Britain. I met him on a few occasions in the BBC where, like myself, he was a regular broadcaster from the Religious Department. He was a most gentle, learned and spiritual man. He always spoke to me about life in Northern Ireland. He was fascinsated and puzzled by the violence of so called Christians.

More than anybody, Zaki Badawi is responsible for establishing a modern Islam that fits easily with British society. He founded a Muslim College in Britain and took part in interfaith discussions among Muslims, Christians and Jews. He spent his life resolving problems within his Muslim community and being a reasonable, rational and acceptable voice for the Muslim community throughout the world. Against all the fundamentalists he held that Islam is a universal religion with many valid cultural manifestations.

He worked hard so that people coming from India and Pakistan could adapt to British cultures and British civilisation and still remain good Muslims. He coined the phrase 'British Muslims'.

11 February

Psychologists say we can make life easier for ourselves and others by following a few simple guidelines on happiness.

For example, we should learn to count our blessings. Once a week take time to write down three or four things which make you happy. It could be a small thing like seeing a flower bloom or a big thing like seeing your child or grandchild take their first steps.

Virtue and vice become easier with practice. Practising acts of kindness not only helps us to be kind but helps others too. Let somebody go ahead of you in the queue at the supermarket or coming out of a side road in traffic. Prepare a lunch for an old person who wouldn't otherwise get one. Recognising that we can be of help to others, boosts our own happiness.

Enjoy the pleasures of life. If you get a delightful dinner today, enjoy every morsel of it. Take mental pictures of pleasurable moments and play them over in your mind.

12 February

The American Bishops set up a National Review Board to plan a way ahead for the American Church. They reported back in February 2004. It was an excellent report. So good that it has been ignored ever since.

Here's a quote from it: 'The exercise of authority without accountability is not servant leadership; it is tyranny.' That's it in a nutshell – and a tyranny cannot be from God.

When I examine my own conscience, I have to admit that we priests urgently need to learn how to listen. We need to listen not just to answer questions, but listen so that we may be transformed as well as informed.

There is little inspirational leadership in church circles these days and it is only when dedicated lay leaders collaborate with open-minded clergy that we can overcome this crisis of trust.

13 February

Gratitude is a way of boosting your happiness. If somebody has helped you, tell them so. Don't wait until they're dead. Brighten their life now.

Learn to forgive. Somebody once told me that holding on to resentment is like taking poison yourself and waiting for your enemy to die.

Take time for special people in your life like family and friends. Strong personal relationships are the best antidote to loneliness. We have to invest time in relationships.

Take care of yourself. It's good to get sleep, exercise, food and rest.

Have personal mental strategies to help you cope with stress. Little phrases like 'that which doesn't kill me makes me stronger'; or Roy Keane's famous one 'if you fail to prepare, you prepare to fail' are helpful. Obviously for me, religious faith helps me through the difficult times of life.

And finally here's one I've told you before but it bears repeating. 'Each of us will have to answer to God for the permissible pleasures in life that we failed to enjoy.' Now when was the last time a preacher told you that pleasure wasn't a sin?

14 February

There is a line in the sand which cannot be crossed. Bank robbing, drug dealing, punishment beatings, murder, are the wrong side of the line. That's criminal activity and those who do it are criminals, plain and simple. No cause justifies the cover-up. No cause is served by denial of the obvious.

It takes a long time to build up trust. But once it is broken it is never regained – ever. The church discovered that to its cost.

15 February

'If there's one art form which has been consistently used to draw me to God, it is music. Music feeds my soul. It delights my heart and so often speaks to me the things of God. Sometimes it simply transports me to a glimpse of heaven … If sloth is nothing less than the loss of the sense of wonder, then music is an antidote to sloth. This can be the power of music.

It can thrill and delight us, not just in the sense that it has an emotional impact, but in the way it can change our view of life. It can involve us in a movement of the soul. It can be purposefully used as an introduction to prayer. It can, indeed, become prayer. It can be the means by which God speaks to us directly and clearly …' (*Breathing I Pray*, by Ivan Mann, Darton Longman Todd, 2005.)

16 February

Are you inspired by this statement? 'The laity are entitled, and indeed sometimes duty bound, to express their opinion on matters which concern the good of the church.' A radical theologian? Not at all. That's paragraph 37 of the *Dogmatic Constitution on the Church*.

What I have been writing recently is upsetting to a small section of concerned readers. I don't mean to upset anyone. I try to express my views as honestly as I can. But I am quite aware that I have no right to deliberately take away another's peace so that I can claim honesty. I have a duty, according to the official documents of the church, to express an opinion. And I try to do it in an acceptable rather than controversial way.

I believe the church is always in need of ongoing reform and renewal. I also believe that silence and secrecy are at the root of the problems the church is experiencing at the present time.

I have noticed a new trend in clerical circles. Even the most hard line are beginning to recognise that we have a problem, although many people feel that our problems should not be discussed in public. I know it's a ridiculous point of view to hold, but let's try to be gentle with the slow learners.

What many hard liners are not prepared to admit though, is that the institutional church has to examine its structures critically.

17 February

I was at a very pleasant function recently when Albert and Kathleen Reynolds were honoured by The Charity for Children in Dublin Castle.

Ireland's Charity for Children was set up less than three years ago and has managed to bring Telemedicine facilities to 42 hospitals all over Ireland, North and South.

Through Telemedicine a doctor can examine patients via a tele-link and can make use of the best knowledge, the best expertise and the best equipment from around the world. It's particularly helpful in diagnosing specific forms of cancer and recommending the proper treatment.

The foundation first set up a link between Our Lady's Hospital for Sick Children in Crumlin and St Jude's Children's Hospital in Memphis Tennessee, probably the most successful hospital in the world for the treatment and management of cancer in children.

Later Ireland's Charity for Children installed Telemedicine equipment in every children's unit in Northern Ireland and in the Republic of Ireland. As a result the lives of many children have been saved.

18 February

In the current issue of *Intercom*, 'A Pastor' writes his last article. This is how he finishes:

'Trying to undo the damage of my Maynooth days and most of my priesthood when the practice of religion diminished me, stunted me, dehumanised me … Religion for me now is not discovering this truth or finding that meaning. It is about living as fully as possible in the present moment, and finding echoes of a longing for the sacred in the ordinariness of things: the beauty of a rose, the laughter of a child …. Above all, it is a gathering sense of God's presence in my life, not because I have managed to find my way through the maze of a snakes-and-ladders morality where sin and virtue demand pre-packaged responses, but because I have come to a place where I sense that, extraordinarily and disconcertingly, God actually loves me. There is no other place I want to be.'

19 February

One of the most peaceful places on earth for me is Lourdes. And apart from the Grotto area, which for me is heaven on earth, the most wonderful place in Lourdes is the City of the Poor. Only one quarter of Irish pilgrims ever visit it, which is a pity. The City of the Poor is many things. It's a hostel where 500 people can stay in a respectful and dignified way for their pilgrimage. There are about 30 permanent staff who run it and there are about 1000 volunteers who give up two to three weeks of their free time every year to keep the City of the Poor open 24 hours a day for 11 months of the year. It is also about a beautiful small little sheepfold church which seats 60 people and where I have been lucky enough to celebrate some of the most meaningful Masses of my priestly life.

The City of the Poor is situated well away from the rush of the normal pilgrim. It was founded at the request of St Bernadette herself and often welcomes 20,000 pilgrims a year who are wounded by life and come to Lourdes looking for hope. It's especially for those people who wouldn't be able to afford the normal pilgrimage but who would still want to go to Lourdes in search of hope.

20 February

I have a little problem. Little is the correct word. My problem is that I can't determine whether spectacles or umbrellas are the most frequently lost items in the world. In our church we can pick up ten pairs of spectacles a week. Nobody ever comes back for them.

But ours is nothing compared to what they find on trains and buses in big cities. The London Underground say that 140,000 items are left on trains each year. The most common lost items there are cases and bags. They pick up 24,000 a year and most of them are never claimed. Mobile phones and umbrellas come second. Just over 8,000 of each. They have to dispose of 6,000 pairs of spectacles and 8,000 sets of keys every year. And according to their press officer, over the years the following items have been left on trains – a human brain, a jar full of bull's sperm, prosthetic limbs, wedding dresses, a stuffed eagle, a grandfather clock, an Elvis suit and, most amazingly of all, breast implants.

When I read that I was quite happy to deal with spectacles and umbrellas.

21 February

Fr Donald Cozzens has been a priest for nearly 40 years. At present he is a Director of Religious Studies and Writer in Residence at the John Carroll University in Cleveland. But previously he was Rector of a Seminary in Ohio, a Vicar for Diocesan priests, a professor, a psychologist, and a theologian. He's a heavyweight.

However, Donald Cozzens is always reasonable and calm in what he says. He admits celibacy has a huge fascination for the media. There is a spiritual aura around celibates, ordained or lay, who are comfortable in their single status. Those who have the gift of celibacy are at home with themselves. 'For those gifted with the charism, it is a blessing, it is their truth, and the key to their spiritual freedom. But for those normal healthy men who lack the charism it is a burden which can become a silent martyrdom,' he writes.

Cozzens even suggests that there could be benefits from abolishing celibacy. One of those would be the values women bring to a relationship. 'What it desperately needs is the voice and influence of the feminine, embodied in the lives of today's women of the church. A married clergy would bring us closer to that reality.'

22 February

'To delight in war is a merit in the soldier, a dangerous quality in the captain, and a positive crime in the Statesman.'
(George Santayana)

23 February

Rabbi Harold Kushner wrote a little gem of a book called, *When Bad Things Happen To Good People*. In case you haven't read it, Kushner's little boy died after years of suffering and even though he was a devout Rabbi he simply couldn't cope. He had to take time off to unravel the mystery of why suffering is so unfair.

He writes: 'I have seen people made noble and sensitive through suffering, but I have also seen people go cynical and bitter. If God is testing us, he must know by now that many of us fail the test. The various responses to tragedy all assume that God is the cause of our suffering. But maybe our suffering happens for some reason other than the will of God ... Could it be that God does not cause the bad things that happen to us? Could it be that he does not decide which families should give birth to handicapped children, but rather, that he stands ready to help us cope with our tragedies?

'One day, a year and a half after Aaron's death, I realised that I had gone beyond self-pity to accepting what had happened. I knew that no-one ever promised us a life free from disappointment. The most anyone promised was that we would not be alone in our pain, that we would be able to draw upon a source outside ourselves for strength and courage. I now recognise that God does not cause our misfortunes, but helps us – by inspiring other people to help.'

24 February

'Hope is what sits by a window and waits for one more dawn, despite the fact that there isn't an ounce of proof in tonight's black sky that it can possibly come.'
(Joan Chittister)

25 February

Tight tabloid writing is as old as time itself and is the most effective and lasting way to communicate. For example:

In Lord's Prayer there are 56 words.

The Lord Is My Shepherd has 118 words.

The Gettysburg Address has 226 words.

The Ten Commandments have 297 words.

But a recent US Department of Agriculture Order on the price of cabbage contained just over 16,000 words.

26 February

Since 1945 more than 23 million deaths have been caused by war.

During the 1990s, 90% of the casualties of war were civilians.

In the last ten years over 3 million children have been killed in armed conflict,

8 million disabled and 15 million children left homeless.

400,000 children around the world are fighting the wars of adults presently.

In the 1900s there were more deaths through conflict than in all the other centuries put together.

27 February

An Anglican clergyman, the Rev William Archibald Spooner, is regarded as the all-time champion of the verbal blooper. He was warden of New College Oxford. He was a nervous man who had trouble getting his words to come out straight.

In church one Sunday, Spooner told his congregation: 'Let us sing, 'The Kinkering Congs Their Tattles Tike.' The hymn was: 'The Conquering Kings Their Titles Take.'

At a wedding he told the groom, 'It is kistomary to cuss the bride.'

Calling on the dean of Christ Church, he asked the secretary 'Is the bean dizzy?' Giving the eulogy at a clergyman's funeral, he praised his departed colleague as a 'shoving leopard to his flock.' (i.e. loving shepherd).

In another sermon he warned his congregation: 'There is no peace in a home where dinner swells.' He intended to say 'where a sinner dwells.'

Speaking to a group of farmers, Spooner intended to greet them as 'sons of toil' but said, 'I see before me tons of soil.'

28 February

In the temptation in the wilderness Jesus is trying to discover his true self. So when we don't know who we are, we are liable to fall to deception and temptation. Temptation often appears as our fantasy selves. We begin to think of what we could be or should be. But Jesus in the wilderness finds his true self and he learns a number of things. He learns:

a) Despite the devil's promise he will be empty. He will be hungry. But he also learns that he will still be God's beloved Son. Unlike the devil, God will still love us anyway.

b) He learns that he will suffer. And he knows that even in his suffering God is with him. Suffering is not a punishment. He will still be a beloved child, even when he suffers.

c) In the wilderness with his true self he discovers that power in itself is useless. The more powerless he feels the more redemption comes. And once again he will still be loved anyway even without power.

That's what Jesus discovered in his time in the wilderness.

29 February

Over 75 years ago a young genius named Philo T. Farnsworth devised a system to transmit a series of lines through the air which could form a picture. Even as a 14-year-old boy growing up in Idaho, he sketched a diagram which showed that images could be reproduced by shooting a beam of electrons against a light sensitive screen. His High School science teachers luckily had some idea what he was trying to achieve.

After six years of research, experimentation and many failures, the breakthrough came about on 7 September 1927. He managed to transmit a single white line unto a screen in his laboratory. At that moment Farnsworth had invented the television.

Because of that breakthrough many other engineers, technicians and scientists developed highly sophisticated technologies that have made television the force it is today. Sadly, because there have been so many stunning advances, Farnsworth's contribution has largely been forgotten.

But there was one occasion which made Farnsworth immensely proud and rightly so. It was on that historic day in July 1969 when the technology he created made it possible to see Neil Armstrong walk on the moon. On that night Farnsworth turned to his wife and said, 'This has made it all worthwhile.'

1 March

Spreading the Good News is part of every Christian's life at Easter. Jesus is risen from the dead. Here are 20 suggestions:

1. Brighten up. Put your biggest worry in God's hands.
2. Read a child a story about the first Easter.
3. Thank people who have helped you on your faith journey. Tell them what they said or did which affected you.
4. How has God gifted you? Use that talent to make a difference to somebody's life.
5. Be generous to your community. Share your time, your skills, money or possessions.
6. Have a look at how you work. Be more just and life-giving.
7. Explain to a friend the reasons you believe.
8. Thank somebody who has a tedious job, e.g. the car park attendant, the girl at the checkout counter, the person in the restaurant.
9. Look at the subtle ways you keep somebody dependent and powerless. How can you change, to affirm that person's worth?
10. Count your blessings and then tell them to another.
11. Say thanks to a suffering person for the way they have persevered in hope and for the special witness they offer you.
12. Make up for the back biting spiral that goes on by affirming other people's qualities in your own conversation as often as possible.
13. Romance your spouse or girlfriend/boyfriend in a special way.
14. Give up a destructive habit, for example, running yourself down, and replace it with a positive one, e.g. affirmation of self.
15. Listen – really listen to someone you thought you knew already. Discover yet another God-given uniqueness about him/her and say what it is.
16. Think what a great gift faith is. Let go of a long standing grudge.
17. Put your self in another's shoes. Work hard at overcoming a deeply ingrained prejudice.
18. Contemplate the gift of health and make the most of it.
19. Be pro-life by praising the parent, welcoming a child or offering help to a pregnant mum or an expectant dad.
20. Last, but not least, try thanking a tired priest.

2 March

Anthony Mastroem wrote the following provocative comment:

No one steals anymore ... they simply lift something.

No one lies anymore ... they simply misrepresent the facts.

No one commits adultery ... they simply play or fool around.

No one kills an unborn baby ... they simply terminate a pregnancy.

All of this, says Maestroem, is simply a clever, if dishonest way, of candy-coating the reality of sin.

- If God wanted a permissive society, he would have given us Ten suggestions, instead of Ten Commandments.
- Calling a spade 'an agricultural implement' does nothing to change what it is!

3 March

On Sunday morning he is sitting in church with his family. On Monday morning he and his partners are making promises to customers they know they can never keep. He gets the contracts but doesn't see the contradiction between Sunday and Monday in his life.

She's a member of the choir. After singing God's praises she and her friends meet for lunch and tear another member's character to pieces. The Jesus she serves in praise and song is betrayed over a bottle of white wine and salad.

We know the Creed by heart and wouldn't think of missing Mass. But we walk by the homeless person with the outstretched hand, without ever noticing him.

4 March

This was written by 8 year old, Danny Dutton of Chula Vista, CA, for his third grade homework assignment. The assignment was to explain God:

'One of God's main jobs is making people. He makes them to replace the ones that die, so there will be enough people to take care of things on earth. He doesn't make grownups, just babies. I think because they are smaller and easier to make. That way he doesn't have to take up his valuable time teaching them to talk and walk. He can just leave that to mothers and fathers.

God's second most important job is listening to prayers. An awful lot of this goes on, since some people, like preachers and things, pray at times beside bed time. God doesn't have time to listen to the radio or TV because of this. Because he hears everything, there must be a terrible lot of noise in his ears, unless he has thought of a way to turn it off.

God sees everything and hears everything and is everywhere which keeps him pretty busy. So you shouldn't go wasting his time by going over your mom and dad's head asking for something they said you couldn't have.

Jesus is God's Son. He used to do all the hard work like walking on water and performing miracles and trying to teach the people who didn't want to learn about God. They finally got tired of him preaching to them and they crucified him. But he was good and kind, like his Father, and he told his Father that they didn't know what they were doing and to forgive them and God said OK.

His dad (God) appreciated everything that he had done and all his hard work on earth so he told him he didn't have to go out on the road anymore. He could stay in heaven. So he did. And now he helps his dad out by listening to prayers and seeing things which are important for God to take care of and which ones he can take care of himself without having to bother God. Like a secretary, only more important.'

5 March

I had a helpful letter from a Samaritans member:

Samaritans believe that acts of self harm – sometimes, when more serious, thought of as attempted suicide – are silent screams and attempts to deal with emotional pain. Every statement of an intent to take one's own life or an actual attempt should be taken seriously.

Our reaction to those who have survived a suicide attempt or who are discovered to be self-harming on an ongoing basis, is absolutely crucial. Samaritans believe that a response offering a chance for emotions to be expressed openly, safely and fully is a good way to start dealing with a personal crisis.

Even though every suicide is a tragedy for the individual, family and community, the burning issue is suicide among younger people. Family dynamics will often not lend themselves to such an expression of emotions – particularly if there has been the trauma of a suicide attempt.

Samaritans and other helplines exist to help in a crisis when it's impossible to talk about it with anyone known to the person. Samaritans volunteers all over Ireland urge people to remember that Samaritans is a phone call or email away.

6 March

According to the BBC the seven deadly sins are out of date. To save your embarrassment the seven deadly sins as of old were these: Anger, pride, envy, gluttony, lust, sloth and greed.

According to the BBC's survey on their *Heaven and Earth* show, very few people think that is a list of sins at all. Only 9% said they had been guilty of committing any of those sins. They must be saints. Of those who admitted giving in to one of the deadly sins, 79% gave way to anger. Followed by pride, envy, lust, sloth and only 54% admitted to the sin of greed.

Not unexpectedly, lust was the sin that both men and women said they would enjoy most. Surprisingly gluttony was a popular sin with women, but not with men.

7 March

Here's a thought for Lent. It is only recently I became aware of the term, 'The spirituality of subtraction'. It means that rather than adding on extra devotions, we should in fact have less and less things which distract us from the centre of the spiritual life, namely God.

Fr Richard Rohr puts it well. 'The spiritual life has much more to do with subtraction than it does with addition. Yet I think Christians today are involved in great part in a spirituality of addition. The capitalist world is the only world most of us have ever known. We see reality, experiences, events, other people, things – in fact everything – as objects for consumption. The nature of the capitalist mind is that things (often people) are there for me. Finally, even God becomes an object of our consumption.' (Richard Rohr, *Letting Go*) If you thought about that long enough, you'd be on the road to a happier life.

8 March

1. Jesus, God's suffering servant, was there. 'They crucified him.'
2. Jesus, the man of prayer, was there. 'Father, forgive them.'
3. Jesus, the merciful, was there. 'They don't know what they're doing.'
4. Jesus, the friend of sinners, was there. 'Two robbers were crucified with him.'
5. Jesus, the rejected King, was there. 'This is Jesus, the king of the Jews.'
6. Jesus, the kind man was there. 'Lord, remember me when you come into your kingdom.'
7. Jesus, the man, was there. 'I'm thirsty.'
8. Jesus, the son of Mary, was there. 'Mother, behold your son.'
9. Jesus, the Son of God, was there. 'Father, into your hands I commit my spirit.'
10. Jesus, the ransom for our sins, was there. 'My God, my God, why have you forsaken me?'
11. Jesus, the perfect Saviour, was there. 'It is finished.'
12. Jesus, the victor over death, was there. 'Today, you will be with me in paradise'.

Jesus, the judge of all, was not there. No word of condemnation.
(Abridged from Gordon Harmon)

9 March

Wisdom from Grandpa

Whether a man winds up with a nest egg, or a goose egg, depends a lot on the kind of chick he marries. Trouble in marriage often starts when a man gets so busy earnin' his salt, that he forgets his sugar.

Too many couples marry for better or for worse, but not for good.

When a man marries a woman, they become one. The trouble starts when they try to decide which one.

If a man has enough horse sense to treat his wife like a thoroughbred, she will never turn into an old nag.

On anniversaries, the wise husband always forgets the past – but never the present.

A foolish husband says to his wife, 'Honey, you stick to the washin', ironin', cookin', and scrubbin'. No wife of mine is gonna work.'

The bonds of matrimony are a good investment only when the interest is kept up.

Many girls like to marry a military man – he can cook, sew, make beds, is in good health, and he's already used to taking orders.

Eventually you will reach a point when you stop lying about your age, and start bragging about it.

You know you are getting old when everything either dries up or leaks.

I don't know how I got over the hill without ever getting to the top.

One of the many things no one tells you about aging is that it is such a nice change from being young.

Ah, being young is beautiful, but being old is comfortable.

Old age is when former classmates are so grey and wrinkled and bald, they don't recognise you.

If you don't learn to laugh at trouble, you won't have anything to laugh at when you are old.

10 March

According to the BBC's survey on their *Heaven and Earth* show, attitudes towards sin have changed. Now we're more concerned with actions which hurt other people, rather than the seven deadly sins.

The new list of deadly sins according to the people asked in this survey are: 1.Cruelty; 2. Hypocrisy; 3. Selfishness; 4. Greed; 5. Dishonesty; 6. Bigotry and 7. Adultery. You notice that greed is on both the old and new lists. In fact, it could be argued that the new list is really the same list with a different emphasis. By any standards there's a close connection between lust and adultery. And there's a strong case to be made that the basis of all sin is selfishness. What I'm delighted about is that people still think sin exists.

I wonder what your list would be? But before you start writing them, remember that as soon as you point a finger at anybody else, three fingers point back at yourself.

11 March

We all burn energy making martyrs of ourselves. Worse still are the 'if only' brigade. It's as simple as this. What has happened can't be undone. So don't make things worse by throwing a good life after a bad one. There's not a person on earth who doesn't wish that they had lived life differently. But there's no point doing your head in fighting against reality. Make up your mind to let things go. That way you give yourself permission to have a fresh start.

Don't make the same mistakes over and over again. If something goes wrong think about it, spot where it went wrong, then take some action to ensure it doesn't go wrong next time. If you have made a mess of things and said something stupid to another person, don't let it simmer. Say sorry, admit your mistake, it won't kill you. When you are up front about it you can leave your mistakes behind you. It's not the mistake which is the problem, but how you handle it.

12 March

Be grateful. Those who are grateful for their gifts are always more positive than those who spend their lives complaining about gifts they don't have. Take time to think about what you have and be grateful for it.

Like yourself. It seems obvious when you say it. If you don't like yourself, why should anybody else like you? There will be things about yourself that you don't like. Then change them. Don't use them as an excuse to hate yourself. I have always found it useful to list five gifts and then try to prioritise them. Another tip is to do something enjoyable every day. If you keep putting off what you enjoy, then you will never find time for it. Likewise if you have a list of problems, try and sort at least one of them today. Make the most of your opportunities and never stop working on yourself to be better.

13 March

Terry Wogan hasn't lost his sense of humour. According to a recent column, in *Woman's Weekly*, he was involved in payola when he worked with RTÉ. Payola in those days was called dropsie. (You dropped the disc jockey a few quid for himself to play your record. Drop. Dropsie? Get it?) This is how Terry remembers it.

'One afternoon when I was preparing the running order for the show, (Hospital Requests) a manager of one of the most popular showbands looked around the open door of the office. Civil greetings were exchanged, and after the statutory ten minutes of pointless blather, the reason for his visit became plain. He had the latest record of his band, especially for me. He wanted me to listen to it, because he respected my opinion above all others, and he personally would be amazed if I didn't think it was the finest thing of its kind since Count John McCormack kicked the bucket! A natural for Hospital Requests and a crowd pleaser that would have the patients leaping from their beds. I said I would certainly give it a listen, and, shaking his hand, I excused myself to the bathroom. Luckily, I had finished my simple toilet, when your man entered. He moved swiftly, even surreptitiously to my side. 'Now,' he said as he pressed a packet of 20 Navy Cut into my hand, 'that's for yourself.' He left as swiftly as he had come. I never played the record. I can't be bought!'

14 March

A poor woman carrying a small pail came to Mother Teresa's soup kitchen to beg for rice for her children. Mother Teresa took her small pail and filled it with rice from the kitchen's bin. After thanking Mother for her kindness, the woman took out a second container and poured half of the rice into it. 'Why did she do that?' Mother Teresa was asked by a visitor. Mother explained that the second container was for another family near the woman's home who could not make the long trek to the soup kitchen. Why, then, did she not offer to fill the second container for the woman? Mother Teresa answered, 'Because I did not want to deprive her of the blessing of sharing.'

15 March

- You come quietly into my private world and let me be.
- You really try to understand me when I do not make much sense.
- You don't take my problem from me, but trust me to deal with it in my own way.
- You give me enough room to discover for myself why I feel upset, and enough time to think for myself what is best.
- You allow me the dignity of making my own decisions even though you feel I am wrong.
- You don't tell me that funny story you are just bursting to tell me.
- You allow me to make my experience one that really matters.
- You accept my gratitude by telling me that it is good to know I have been helped.
- You grasp my point of view even when it goes against your sincere convictions.
- You accept me as I am – warts and all.
- You don't offer me religious solace when you sense I am not ready for it.
- You look at me, feel for me, and really want to know me.
- You spend a short, valuable time with me and make me feel it is for ever.
- You hold back your desire to give me good advice.

16 March

When you have bishops and less worthy clerics, pontificating about 'Living in sin', and 'No right to go to communion', then anyone who has to wait five years for their Annulment Papers to be looked at is being dealt with unjustly. It's a basic principle that justice delayed is justice denied.

Those causing people to be deprived of the Eucharist will have a harsher judgement than the couple who recognised their love as a wonderful gift from God, and accepted it graciously.

17 March

St Patrick was insistent that there should be one Lord, one faith, one baptism. And that nothing was impossible to God – a God he himself prayed to 100 times a day.

This morning, perhaps one of Patrick's own prayers for peace and protection in a time of strife would be appropriate:

May the strength of God guide me this day.
May his power preserve me.
May the wisdom of God instruct me.
And the ear of God hear me.
The hand of God defend me.
And may Christ protect me against an untimely death.

A relevant prayer indeed.

18 March

There was a mother who had three very successful sons. And they decided to make her birthday very special for her. The first one was a very builder so he bought a huge mansion for his mother. There were nine bedrooms in it, twelve bathrooms, garages and God knows what. The second son thought he would buy her a top of the range Mercedes. The third brother knew his mother was religious so he decided to get her something special. He travelled the world and eventually found this rare and wonderful parrot. This parrot could repeat verses from the Bible at random.

A month later they came back and each wanted to know how his present had been received. The mother said to the first one, well the house was beautiful, but I have discovered I can only sleep in one room at a time. And all these rooms have to be cleaned. My old little house could be done in a half hour. I wish I were back in my old house. To the second son who bought the Mercedes, she said, it is a beautiful car and it is very comfortable. But I'm afraid I'll scratch it. I was far more comfortable in my own banger. To the third son she said, I have to say it was a wonderful present, because that little bird you bought me was the tastiest bit of chicken I have ever eaten in my life.

19 March

Just because it looks weird don't discard it. Believe it or not, you can read it:

I cdnuolt blveiee taht I cluod aulaclty
uesdnatnrd waht I was rdgnieg. The
phaonmneal pweor of the hmuan mnid. Aoccdrnig to
rscheearch at Cmabrigde
U'inervtisy, it deosn't mttaer in waht oredr the
ltteers in a wrod are,
the olny iprmoatnt tihng is taht the frist and lsat
ltteer be in the rghit
pclae. The rset can be a taotl mses and you can
sitll raed it wouthit a
porbelm. Tihs is bcuseae the huamn mnid deos not
raed ervey lteter by
istlef, but the wrod as a wlohe. Amzanig huh?

46

20 March

You might not be familiar with the name Archbishop Paul Marcinkus but he was for many years the Pope's bodyguard. I met him on numerous occasions when Pope John Paul II came to Ireland in September 1979. Marcinkus then was at the height of his power. A gigantic 6' 4" bald-headed all-powerful Vatican cleric, he had all the arrogance of a Chicago crook, which many people thought he was.

He was involved in the huge Vatican bank scandal which ultimately led to the death of Roberto Calvi who was found hanging under Black Friars Bridge in London in 1982. Because of the debt the Vatican bank got into, Marcinkus was held responsible and eventually he became too hot to handle. He was removed from office and was a virtual prisoner for most of his life.

At the end of his days he became chaplain to 20 Golf Clubs in Arizona. Maybe he was happy there.

Either way he's a perfect example of what happens career clerics. The system uses and disposes at will. You can be all-powerful while you support the institution but as soon as you become an embarrassment you are ignominiously discarded. It's hard to find Christ in church politics.

21 March

It's a daily ritual for me here in Northern Ireland to meet people wrestling with the impossibility of forgiveness. After decades of brutality and evil, it's not surprising. It's a running sore that won't be easily healed and, if not dealt with, will poison all attempts at peace.

I've come to the conclusion that forgiveness is a journey. It's not a once-off decision to pretend that I don't have my feelings, or that something awful didn't happen. It's a realisation that it is okay to feel angry and bitter, but sooner or later you see the sense of the principle: To feed your own bitterness is like taking poison yourself whilst expecting your enemy to die.

The struggle for forgiveness is at best a one-day-at-a-time journey. And it's for life!

22 March

At long last the real state of church vocations is beginning to impinge. In 2005, 135 priests and brothers and 270 nuns died. 8 were ordained to replace them. The average age of Irish priests is now 61.

No wonder Martin Kennedy, a leading layman who was a parish co-ordinator in Tullamore, says we should have a full scale missionary drive to train lay people to run the numerous priest-less parishes we'll have within the next decade.

23 March

There aren't many letters which bring me to tears. But I got one during the week which had me struggling and still does. I can't quote directly from the letter because the priest who wrote it wants to keep his anonymity and I want to respect his request.

He cannot agree with me that we priests should feel a collective guilt for the sins of other priests. He detests the pain inflicted on innocent children, but he himself has always tried to carry out his duties and tasks as well as he could, respecting the dignity of each person.

Now he has lost hope in the church and institution that he had given his life to. He finds it a cold and unloving place. He agrees with the guidelines that are there to protect children and he agrees, at least in part, that the practice in the past was wrong and should never be repeated again. What he cannot agree with is the proposed sanctions against a priest when an accusation is made. He considers them medieval and ruthless.

'Why should priests be the only people to be hounded by the media, abandoned by their boss, and sometimes by their families and friends, and kicked out of their houses while the alleged accusation is still under investigation?'

Be kind to the kind and encourage the lost, especially if he's your local priest.

24 March

Oscar Romero was Archbishop of San Salvador for just three years. When he was appointed in 1977 he was known as a pious, conservative bishop who wouldn't rock the boat. He changed when his friend Rutilio Grande, a Jesuit priest, was murdered because of his commitment to the poor. His friend's death transformed Romero from a timid, conventional cleric to an outspoken champion of justice, and the first bishop to be murdered at the altar since Thomas Beckett in the 12th century.

In his weekly broadcast sermons, Romero highlighted social injustices, stood up for the poor and denounced corrupt leaders. He was accused by his fellow bishops and the ruling elite of subordinating the gospel to politics. But Romero answered by pointing to the courage of the poor and saying, 'With these people it is not hard to be a Good Shepherd.'

On the day before his death he appealed to soldiers to disobey illegal orders. 'The peasants you kill are your own brothers and sisters. When you hear the voice of a man commanding you to kill, remember instead the voice of God. "Thou shalt not kill".'

The next day as he was offering Mass, a single rifle shot was fired from the rear of the church. Romero was struck in the heart and died within minutes on 24 March 1980.

25 March

Ten ways to avoid life's tribulations:
1. Take a pen to the bank.
2. Take toilet paper to the pub.
3. Never book a flight on Bank Holidays.
4. Get a gas barbecue.
5. Wear earplugs in the dentist's waiting room.
6. Take your own radio when staying in hotels.
7. Give up supporting whatever team frustrates.
8. Rent a video if you are planning to watch TV on a Saturday night.
9. Have a decent meal before going to a nouvelle cuisine restaurant.
10. Concrete the garden.

26 March

Saint Charles of Mount Argus I

Mount Argus in Dublin was founded in 1856 but the first Rector died within a few months and that was why Fr Charles was sent over to Dublin to join a very small community of priests and brothers in Harold's Cross. His preaching was poor, his English was worse but in the confessional and blessing the sick he excelled.

He became extraordinarily popular not only in Dublin but all over Ireland through the gift of healing. Records show that as many as 300 people a day came on foot and in carts from Ireland and beyond. But where there's success there's a begrudger. And Blessed Charles met many of them in his life.

Some doctors wrongly claimed that he was advising people not to receive medical attention, and others accused him of being involved in a scam, selling holy water. Even though he was totally innocent, he was banished to England. Mount Argus, which was thriving at the time, pretty much fell apart as soon as he left. He spent eight years in England training novices and doing normal and sometimes insignificant tasks.

27 March

Saint Charles of Mount Argus II

In 1874 he came back to Mount Argus. Again Mount Argus thrived and the huge church and monastery, still on the site to this day, was the fruit of the work of Fr Charles during the last 20 years of his life there.

His own health was failing at this time and the last five years of his life were a trying time for him. He died in January 1893 and his body lay in state for five days in the church. Thousands came to his funeral, one of the biggest ever seen in Ireland at that time. Devotion lasted long after his death and, because so many people thought of him as a saint, his body was exhumed from the graveyard in 1949 and encased in a shrine within the church. There it remained until it was exhumed again for the beatification in October 1988 and a new shrine was built.

28 March

Saint Charles of Mount Argus III

The first miracle certified by the Vatican was that of Mrs Octavia Verheggen. She was a distant relative of Fr Charles but hadn't much faith in him until she herself was near death. In a moment of despair in the middle of the night she cried out, 'Fr Charles, if you are in heaven heal me.' And indeed she was healed and both medical and Vatican experts agreed that it was truly miraculous.

The miracle which made him a saint was the cure of Dolf Dormans who comes from the same little village of Munstergeleen. He is still alive today and goes to Mass daily in the local church. He was given up for dead a couple of years ago. But the Parish Priest of Munstergeleen brought a relic of Blessed Charles to him and blessed him with it in the presence of his family. Mr Dormans had great devotion to Blessed Charles anyway but within a few days he was perfectly cured and doctors operated again to ensure that what they had seen a few weeks earlier had in fact healed. They said his cure could not have been the result of medical science and so the way was opened for the canonisation of Fr Charles.

29 March

Saint Charles of Mount Argus IV

Very shortly we will have a stamp to commemorate his canonisation, and a new portrait by artist James Hanley will be used for that. A number of hymns have been written and there will be pilgrimages to Rome for the canonisation. I won't be there. I'd much rather be where I was on the day of his beatification, in Mount Argus where 'poor aul Charlie' lived and died.

He was an immigrant and an emigrant who spent many a lonely day in Dublin. He lived and worked in Ireland at a time when the faith was not as strong as we sometimes think. But he understood the value of Christ's suffering and death to those who are sick. He himself lived that suffering and was never cured. Through his intercession, many hundreds were healed while he was alive and I can personally testify that many hundreds, even to this day, would attribute their healing to the intercession of the new saint of Mount Argus, poor aul Charlie.

30 March

I was fascinated by a report about a lady called Anne Nelson. She was an important worker for Cantor Fitzgerald, who lost most of their staff in the World Trade Centre. Anne Nelson worked on 'floor 104' and died with her colleagues.

When people were clearing her apartment afterwards, they picked out a few personal belongings and put them in a bag to send to her parents in Dakota. Her parents were coming to terms with their grief and really didn't need this bag of memories. So they put them in the basement and couldn't even look them, never mind touch them. But last summer they realised they were not coping with their grief healthily. They got the strength to go down to the basement and look through some of the physical things their daughter left behind.

One of them was a lap top, which her parents eventually opened. In it they found a list, entitled 'The Top 100'. They thought it was a list of favourite music tracks and that inspired them to flick it open. Instead they found not a list of pop tunes, but a list of goals, she had set herself. Sadly she got only to number 37 in the list when she was cruelly wiped off the face of the earth. She filed her goals under specific headings.

The section which caught my attention was: *How to be a better human being*. In there she resolved to be somebody who can respect the secrets of others. She reminded herself not to be ashamed of who she is and to do things which 'will make me a person to be proud of'. Finally and ironically, she promised herself: 'I should spend more time with my family and make time for my friends.'

31 March

Fr Kieran Creagh was shot four times and left for dead, as he protected his hospice for those dying from AIDS. If we ever design a new priesthood, some DNA from Fr Kieran Creagh would be most helpful. He's the kind of priest we need today.

It was when he went to South Africa that he found his true calling. He recognised that AIDS is destroying the black community, especially the poor black people. And, on his own initiative, he began to think about a hospice which would help those dying from HIV/AIDS related illnesses. With the help of his family and friends he succeeded in building a hospice for 20 people. It's not enough but it is a start.

One of the temptations that face us priests throughout our lives is that we are becoming increasingly irrelevant. It's easy to wonder late at night if we make a difference at all. Well, people like Kieran Creagh do. They make a difference to the people who matter, the poor, the wounded, the dying, the rejected.

Good priests who are different, will always make a difference.

1 April

Pope John Paul II was always in danger of suffering the back lash of his long reign. Had he, for example, died shortly after the time of his attempted assassination, he would now be viewed as a martyr and probably one of the greatest Popes of the modern era.

His life was full of paradoxes. He was the first non-Italian Pope for 400 years, yet acted with the conservatism of a Roman bureaucrat. The greatest influences on his young life were the tyranny of Nazism and the failure of communism, yet he was often accused of dealing with dissent in a way that echoed both tyrannies.

Undoubtedly the world has been an immensely better place because of his reign. His achievement as a politician and human rights activist bears comparison with any leader anywhere in the past 50 years.

An assessment of Pope John Paul II has to be on at least three levels. There was a) Pope John Paul the Theologian, b) Pope John Paul the Politician, c) Pope John Paul the man.

2 April

a) Pope John Paul the Theologian

John Paul the theologian was always controversial. When he was elected Pope, his native Poland was still suffering persecution. His leadership contributed to the communist regime's collapse. It must have been a matter of great sadness to Pope John Paul to see that a free Poland rejected many of his most cherished views.

Many accused him of rolling back the reforms of the Second Vatican Council. Hans Küng, who suffered greatly under the reign of this Pope, called him, 'A spiritual dictator'. Undoubtedly many people have been badly hurt during his term as Pope.

Women are not welcomed within the church as they should be. Many of his statements about women, as with many other issues, have been excellent. In practice, though, there were too many dismissals of the dignity and role of women in church and society.

Priests who resigned from the ministry to marry were, and are, treated pathetically. Those in second relationships, homosexuals, those who in good conscience practice contraception, ecumenists who wish to welcome believing Christians to communion, were just some of the many people cruelly marginalised in recent years.

It is not clear whether the Pope himself was responsible for it, or whether the people he chose to head his departments were.

He had to be a universal Pope and not just of the Western World. But as the head of the Catholic Church it is essential to be in conversation with the world, so that the world can be truly redeemed, and understand the compassion and love of God for all people.

3 April

b) Pope John Paul the Politician

John Paul the politician carries a different assessment. Here he was hugely successful. It is to his eternal credit that he was the one leader in the world who consistently and bravely stood against the war-mongers invading Iraq. He spoke and worked against violence everywhere, including Ireland.

He was a leader of real substance who played a major part in the collapse of communism. Without him the 20th century would have been a poorer era.

He was eventually persuaded that capital punishment was indefensible morally. In the first edition of the *Catechism of The Catholic Church*, there were sections which justified capital punishment. He defended life at its weakest points, before birth and in old age.

The Jewish philosopher Elie Wiesel said that despite a poor beginning he developed a relationship with Jews second only to Pope John XXIII. He witnessed the Holocaust in Poland as a young man and never forgot it. He offered an apology to the Jewish people and made his apology public when he visited the Western Wall. He was the first Pope to speak to 80,000 Muslims in Morocco and the first to enter a Mosque.

These are only some of his achievements during a long reign as an influential leader on the world stage.

4 April

c) Pope John Paul the man

John Paul the man is the most loved of all. The preacher and charismatic leader Billy Graham said, 'He is the greatest of our modern Popes.' Carter, the former President of the USA, said, 'He was the greatest man I have ever met.' Gorbachev said he was, 'One the 20th century's most influential figures.'

As we look forward, it's clear that the church has in a sense stood still for the past ten years. Priests and people have been respectfully waiting for John Paul II to pass on. The world gave him the send-off he truly deserved. But it would be a mistake to see it as an acceptance of the church as it now is. The new Pope will have many years of suffering trying to come to terms with many of the issues which have been left untouched for a decade.

There is a genuine question of credibility in the human institutions of the church. The problem of an aging priesthood is a major issue. And there is an inability to match people's lives with much of what the church teaches.

The leaders he has appointed throughout the world seem incapable of making necessary connections with their flock. And many of the moral answers the church is giving are simply not acceptable to the highly articulate and educated people of the world today.

But back to Pope John Paul. As I look back on his long life, he'll always be the first Pope to visit Ireland. I have no doubt that when the moment of his death came, God welcomed him as a great and faithful servant. A man of his time, a time that is now history.

5 April

We can begin to make our world a better place by standing back from the rat race. A friend offers 7 easy steps to ease away tension:

1. Do nothing.
2. Laugh out loud. Enjoy jokes.
3. Tune into soothing music.
4. Think happy. Imagine a loved one or a peaceful scene.
5. Take a ten minute walk.
6. Inhale and exhale for about five seconds each.
7. Take a few moments to tense and relax your muscles from head to toe.

6 April

At a World Economic Forum in Davos is Switzerland, celebrities took centre stage. At it, Bono made a challenging statement. He said: 'This generation does not want to be remembered solely for inventing the internet. This generation wants to be remembered for trying to do something practical and effective to fight world poverty.' It's an ideal we should support.

I get annoyed when people talk about compassion fatigue. There is no such thing. We should try to help all genuine causes as best we can. We don't live in little boxes. We have a responsibility to help others.

7 April

Make good use of your time by doing good for others and by helping others to do good themselves. It's sound advice and if we want we can always find time. Here are ten simple things each of us could do and which would take up no time at all:

1. Make a conscious effort to smile.
2. Say 'Please', 'Thank you', 'Excuse me'.
3. Give a sincere compliment where it is deserved.
4. Remember someone's name and how to pronounce it.
5. Hold the door open for the person behind you.
6. Let someone with fewer items than you, go ahead of you at the supermarket.
7. Leave a bigger tip than you normally would to somebody who deserves it.
8. Bring a cup of tea or coffee to a colleague.
9. Say 'Good morning' to your co-workers.
10. Do a message for a sick neighbour while you are doing your own.

8 April

A nine year old asked his father, 'Dad, how do wars start?'

'Well, son,' his father began, 'take World War I. That war started when Germany invaded Belgium ...'

'Just a minute,' his wife interrupted. 'It began when Archduke Francis Ferdinand of Austria was assassinated by a Serbian nationalist.'

'Well, dear, that was the spark that ignited the fighting, but the political and economic factors leading to the war had been in place for some time.'

'Yes, I know, honey, but our son asked how the war began and every history book says that World War I began with the murder of Archduke Ferdinand of Austria.'

Drawing himself up with an air of superiority, the husband snapped, 'Are you answering the question, or am I?'

The wife turned her back on him in a huff, stalked out of the room and slammed the door behind her.

When the dishes stopped rattling, an uneasy silence followed. The nine-year-old then broke the silence: 'Dad, you don't have to say any more about how wars start. I understand now.'

9 April

I also believe that younger priests, in Religious Orders in particular, should not be hampered by having to maintain old buildings, old places and old apostolates. The younger men should agree on what kind of Religious Life is relevant to their age. They shouldn't be hampered by old fellows like myself.

Furthermore, we need to look at what the priesthood really means. Do we have to be male celibates? Do we even have to be fulltime? Is there not room for ordaining married men (women) and using the gifts of the laity?

In short, it's time we moved on from the past, it's time we looked at what priesthood really is, because the present priesthood isn't working. It's time we looked at the various human structures and laws within the church which are killing the spirit. We should allow them to die and allow God's Spirit to build a vibrant church which will bring hope instead of despair.

10 April

Moses Maimonides I

I came across a piece written in the twelfth century by the Jewish philosopher Moses Maimonides. He said that there are eight degrees of charity. Here are the first four:

1. The first and the lowest degree is to give, but with reluctance and regret. A gift of the hand but not of the heart.

2. The second is to give cheerfully but not proportionately to the distress of the suffering.

3. The third is to give cheerfully and proportionately but not until we are solicited.

4. The fourth is to give cheerfully, proportionately and even when unsolicited but to put it in the poor man's hand, thereby causing him the painful emotion of shame.

11 April

Here are the rest of them:

5. The fifth is to give charity in such a way that the distressed may receive the bounty and know their benefactor, without being known to him. Such was the conduct of some of our ancestors who used to tie up money in the back pocket of their cloaks so that the poor might take it unnoticed.

6. The sixth, which rises still higher, is to know the object of our bounty but remain unknown to them. Such was the conduct of those of our ancestors who used to convey their charitable gifts into the poor people's dwellings, taking care that their own persons and names should remain unknown.

7. The seventh is better still, namely to give charity in such a way that the giver may not know the relieved persons, nor they the name of the giver.

8. The best way of all is to anticipate charity, by preventing poverty; namely to assist the needy brother or sister either by a considerable gift or a loan of money, or by teaching them a trade or by putting them in the way of business, so that they may earn an honest livelihood and not be forced to the dreadful alternative of holding out his hand for charity. This is the highest step and the best charity of all.

12 April

As Paul Newman explains it, 'It started as a joke and got out of control.' In 1980, the actor and his partner-in-crime, the author A.E. Hotchner, decided to make up Newman's special salad dressing as Christmas gifts for friends. They mixed the ingredients in a wash tub, stirring the concoction with a canoe paddle. Much to their surprise, everyone loved the dressing – and *Newman's Own* was born.

As they readily admit, the company – whose line of products now includes salad dressing, popcorn, lemonade and spaghetti sauce – has succeeded despite their best efforts to mess it up. Thumbing their noses at traditional business marketing techniques and relying instead on instinct, imagination and luck, *Newman's Own* became a premiere name in the food business, with almost $200 million sales every year. Newman and Hotchner give away all the company's after-tax profits for medical research, education, the environment and Newman's special charity, the Hole in the Wall Camps for seriously ill children.

As witnesses of Christ's resurrection, as baptised disciples of his church, we are called to reflect the compassion of God. Whatever 'works' we do – teaching and encouraging, listening and comforting, even making a great salad dressing – can be used for doing great things if we use our gifts for good.

13 April

Last Sunday at Mass I informed my congregation that I was going down to do Podge and Rodge. They howled with laughter. On the way out most of them were not sympathising with me about the death of a dear cousin Packie, but they were sympathising with me about having to appear on Podge and Rodge.

The lead-up to the show was like going to a cross priest in the confessional or a bad dentist who was careless with his drill. The experience itself, however, was very pleasant. As soon as I decided not to take myself too seriously, I remembered that the show belongs to Podge and Rodge, and so let them have all the funny lines. I shouldn't try to take it over. Once that was out of the way I was fine and they treated me a lot better than most television shows do these days.

14 April

It is true that we can't reduce the gospel to a code of what we might call manageable rules for ourselves. Christ didn't come to destroy the Law but he did come to give us ideals which go far beyond laws and rules. 'Be compassionate as your Father is compassionate', was what he said to us. We are pointed in the direction of very high principles. We may never attain them. We shouldn't be disillusioned when we don't. We should be humble enough to accept that we still have the journey to make. Eventually, through the grace of God, we'll get there.

The key word is forgiveness. We need to be able to accept who we really are and forgive ourselves for not being the perfect being we'd love to be. God has no trouble doing it. And it's time we learned that it is his love, not our painful endeavours, which helps us to grow slowly to what we can become.

15 April

Two men were confined to bed in a hospital ward. Both of them were dying. One was beside a window. The other couldn't see out. The one beside the window explained every day what a beautiful place he was looking out on. Manicured lawn, lovely fountain and extravagant flowers. He explained about the young nurses and doctors walking round linking each other in the beauty of the day. The man in the other bed got frustrated that he couldn't see this beautiful scene and was a little jealous. Eventually the man beside the window died and the other man was moved over. When he looked out, with great expectations, to see this beautiful scene, all he saw was a dull concrete wall. The other man used his imagination to think of attractive scenes. In fact the man was blind, but he lived in a world of hope and optimism.

16 April

The God I believe in is a God who excludes no one. He brought people to a banquet and those who didn't want to go were cast aside. It was open to everyone on the highways and byways – no one was excluded.

God is a God who welcomed the prodigal son home, saw him from a long way off and was always looking for him. He didn't take insult. Never listened to a list of sins, but was so glad to see a reconciled heart that he threw a party in his honour. The elder son was miserable about it all. But God had a place in his heart for both of them and he loved both of them. It makes no difference how many times we make mistakes, God always finds something to love in us.

17 April

Ten years ago I suggested that there was no logical or moral reason for banning the use of condoms to prevent the spread of AIDS. In fact, there is a moral obligation to use condoms to protect lives and help prevent the spreading of the killer disease, particularly in the poorer parts of the world. It is based on an accepted moral guideline: where there are two evils, choose the lesser one.

Back then such thinking was roundly condemned by the Vatican statements.

Later leading theologians across the world promoted the idea, which was eventually accepted by a few bishops, particularly in Africa.

Mind you, the church's official line is still to ban under all circumstances the use of condoms, even if they do prevent AIDS. The Vatican still says sexual abstinence is the best way to fight the disease. Everybody agrees that sexual abstinence is the *best* way, but to say it's the *only* way is not sustainable in this day and age.

18 April

God had 99 sheep safe and sound, but wasn't content until he left them all and went out to look for one stray. Nothing is impossible with our God.

God is a God who paid the workers their just wage when they came to work in the vineyard all day, but also gave those who came in the evening the same amount of money. He was making the point that we don't earn it, and God will be generous anyway.

God is a God who made 180 gallons of wine when a few bottles would have done. Nobody can cork God's generosity. There is more than enough for everyone in God's plan.

19 April

Personally I am a great believer in the Twelve Step Recovery Programme for those who are addicted. What I like most about Alcoholics Anonymous or Gambler's Anonymous is that its twelve steps form a practical programme which are simple and wise and which lead to a change of lifestyle, not just a change of habit.

The Twelve Steps as I read them, involve first of all surrendering to God or to a Higher Power because we are not able to cope with our problems ourselves.

Steps 4 to 10 look at how we learn a disciplined and honest way of life, and 11 and 12 deal with spiritual helps to fill the obvious void within us.

It's not only a good programme for the addicted but for any of us. The steps are not a magic cure and they are certainly not easy, but if they are followed carefully and honestly, then they always lead along a healing path.

20 April

God is a God who washed feet. He is a servant God.

God even gave us a final exam in case we'd fail it. 'As long as you do it to the least of my brethren you do it to me.' God is a God who asked only one question of Peter or any of the apostles who abandoned him. The simple question was this, 'Do you love me?' and when they said yes, God loved them in return.

God is a God who died on the cross. He died on a cross with his arms opened wide in love and acceptance. And they are frozen like that for all eternity. By his wounds we are healed.

21 April

There are occasions when an institution can get itself in a total mess trying to defend a position taken at a different time and place by people who thought they knew all the facts. Within the Catholic Church's body of teaching, there are many examples of Vatican documents trying to defend the indefensible out of a loyalty to past statements. It would be more honest to say that those statements were true for their time but are no longer sustainable because of the advance of science, knowledge and human development.

One can only hope for an era of respect for debate. Maybe that will be Pope Benedict's gift to the church today.

22 April

My favourite spiritual writer, Thomas Merton, has said: 'Humility is necessary if we are to avoid acting like babies all our lives and if we are to throw away the illusion that I am the centre of everything.'

23 April

Our God on Calvary is the God of the Accident and Emergency, the AIDS Hospice, the death watcher in hospital and prisons, the homeless lying on the street, the dysfunctional family, the God of failed relationships, sick bodies and broken hearts. This is why Friday is 'Good'. God is always in the darkest places, especially in the places where we are convinced God is absent.

24 April

Charlie Chaplin recalled that his family lived in a world of utter poverty. But the love his mother had for him kept him going. 'I remember an evening in our own room in the basement of Oakley Street. I lay in bed recovering from a fever. Mother and I were alone. It was late afternoon and she sat with her back to the window, reading, acting and explaining the New Testament and Christ's love and pity for the poor and for little children.

'She read well into the night, stopping only to light the lamp. Then she told me of the faith Jesus gave through helping the sick. She described Jesus and his arrest and dignity before Pontius Pilate, in his last agony crying out, "My God, my God, why hast thou forsaken me?"

'Mother had me so convinced that I wanted to die that very night to meet this loving Jesus. But mother said, "Jesus wants you to live first and fulfil your destiny here."

That night left a lasting impression on me.'

25 April

Dr Wilfrid Funk, famous for the dictionaries he composed, once listed the most expressive words in the English language:
1. The most bitter word is 'alone'.
2. The most reverend is 'mother'.
3. The most tragic is 'death'.
4. The most beautiful is 'love'.
5. The most peaceful is 'tranquil'.
6. The saddest is 'forgotten'.
7. The warmest is 'friendship'.
8. The coldest is 'no'.
9. The most comforting is 'faith'.

26 April

PETER: We're having a slight argument.

JESUS: An argument about what?

PETER: About you ... or what you say. We were arguing over which subject you talk about most.

JESUS: Well, which do you think I talk about most?

PETER: I think it must be money ... I reckon you've told more parables to do with money than anything else. There's the Treasure in the Field, the Parable of the Talents, the Rich Fool, the Great Feast, Dives and Lazarus, the Lost Coin ...

JESUS: Come to think of it, I could probably think of another six, but I'm not sure I've told you them all yet.

PETER: Jesus, are you obsessed with money?

JESUS: No ... My parables are not about economics: they're about the kingdom.

PETER: But Jesus, you do talk a lot about money. Think of what you said to the rich young man. You talk more about money than you do about prayer!

JESUS: That may be right, Peter. And if it is, it's because people would rather hear me talking about prayer than about money. Behind a lot of spiritual blindness, and behind a lot of injustice in the world, there's a money problem. And where that's the case, it's safer to talk about your soul than about your finances. But God's interested in what you do with both.

Thanks to Jim Mc C from Cavan for this provocative view of Jesus.

27 April

Recognise yourself?

We are appalled and ashamed at what Judas did but most of us have a few secret pieces of silver in our pocket. Could the reason we show no compassion to people who betray is because we can recognise the Judas chromosome within ourselves?

And before we judge Peter too harshly, remember the sound of the rooster crowing when our silence betrayed someone.

When we disconnect the value of the gospel from the reality of our lives, Judas and Peter take over.

(Anonymous)

28 April

A man from the Midlands writes to me: 'I have always struggled with my faith. I am 43 years of age and a fairly successful business man. At times I have drifted from God but always found my way back. I always attended Sunday Mass with my wife and children, but Mass never 'did it' for me. I don't know why but I rarely connect with the priest.

'I went through many personal struggles – financial, domestic and business worries. What I found always works for me is to visit a church, light a few candles, and try to let my thoughts go before God. In doing this regularly, I find that I am closer to God and will not be led astray.

'Sometimes things happen in the strangest ways but with prayer and faith they always seem to work out.

'Most of our saints who are gone before us must have struggled with their faith also because this life was never meant to be easy. Without God in our lives it would be almost impossible. I am currently going through the biggest personal and moral challenge of my life and I am hoping that with faith, prayer and a few candles, I can come through it. I am confident that I can do it, as I have never been let down yet by God.'

29 April

Although I knew for weeks that Joe Dolan was ill, his death came as a shock. Joe has been part of my life for forty five years and when I visited him in hospital recently, he was still the same Joe – a rock of sense, good humoured and optimistic to a fault.

We talked about sickness, the fragility of life, how it passes whilst we are waiting on it to happen, the precious gift friends are. Then we swapped jokes for twenty minutes. We also said a prayer for healing and I went off into the night happy and all the better for the meeting– the same as I always did when I met Joe. There was no show like a Joe show.

I don't know how we'll manage without Joe. But for today, let's not be greedy. You made all our lives brighter and happier, Joe. May you rest in peace, free from pain and may you be eternally happy. Thanks, Joe. You were a star in every sense of the word. That's why we loved you.

30 April

The Human Condition

Author: 'I am writing a booklet, to be called, *Why Am I Afraid To Tell You Who I Am?'*

Other: 'Do you want an answer to your question?'

Author: 'This is the purpose of the booklet, to answer the question'.

Other: 'But do you want my answer?'

Author: 'Yes, of course I do!'

Other: 'I am afraid to tell you who I am, because, if I tell you who I am, you may not like who I am, and it's all that I have'.

1 May

Three priests got together one day while they were out playing golf. They talked, like most priests do, about deep spiritual matters – the things that really matter. So the conversation most of the day concentrated on how to get bats out of the belfry.

The first priest confessed, 'I have to admit, that even though you are not allowed to destroy bats, I got a gun, through sheer frustration, and fired it at them. All I succeeded in doing was scattering them and making three holes in the ceiling. The bats came back to their home and brought some of their friends as well.'

The second man said he did something that was much more environmentally friendly. He captured the bats in a basket and drove fifty miles. He released them outside an old barn. Unfortunately, when he got home the bats had already arrived back before him.

The third man said he had found the solution to the problem. 'I have no more problems with bats,' he said. 'The first thing I did was baptise them, then I confirmed them. And when I had them baptised and confirmed I never saw them in church from that day to this.'

2 May

For those who would like to lose weight, here is a Dieters' Prayer which has been adapted from *Dr Pickert's Organic Gardening*:

Lord, grant me the strength that I may not fall
Into the clutches of cholesterol
At polyunsaturated, I'll never mutter,
For the road to hell is paved with butter.
And cake is cursed, and cream is awful
And Satan is hiding in every waffle.
Beelzebub is himself a chocolate drop,
And Lucifer is a lollipop.
Teach me the evils of hollandaise, of pasta and gobs of mayonnaise.
And crisp fried chicken from the south –
Lord, if you love me, shut my mouth.

3 May

In an article in the *National Catholic Reporter*, John L. Allen described what it was like working through the night for CNN on the night of Pope John Paul's death. 'Oddly enough, having prepared for these experiences, night and day, for more than five years, having run through endless scenarios on both logistical and journalistic fronts, the one thing I never accounted for was that I would have a personal, emotional response.

'After all a man died, not just any man – John Paul loomed incredibly large in my life. I met him eight times, travelled with him to 21 nations and probably wrote millions of words about him. While I realise there are reasonable criticisms to be made about his papacy, what is beyond question is that he was a man of deep faith and integrity, a genuinely good person striving by his lights to serve God, the church and all of humanity. His final days taught me, and taught all of us, how to face impending death with both grit and grace. And it's a lesson I will never forget … I had to choke back tears, realising in an instant that I would never write another sentence about John Paul II in the present tense.'

It's nice to know that journalists have a heart.

4 May

Somebody sent me one of those inspirational cards recently. It said, *God wants spiritual fruits; not religious nuts.* That's good advice. We can waste a lot of energy doing so-called 'religious' things. God would much prefer us to help our neighbour in a practical way.

Speaking of nuts, reminds me of the man who visited his elderly relative in the Nursing Home. She was sleeping gently so he waited beside her bed. There was a bowl of nuts on her table. Fatally, he took one and before long he'd finished the lot. He had to own up when she awoke. 'I'm sorry auntie, I've eaten all your nuts,' he said apologetically. 'Oh don't worry, James,' she said. 'Once I've sucked the chocolate off them, I don't eat the nuts anyway.'

We're back to spiritual fruits and religious nuts again.

5 May

Cancer I

What's the best way to react when someone you know has cancer? What can you say? What can you do? If I knew the answer I wouldn't make as many mistakes as I do. I often write down a list of 'dos' and 'don'ts' for myself and I'll share some with you today.

Many people still hear the diagnosis of cancer as a death sentence. Which means the person struggling with cancer has a whole new set of values, a whole new lifestyle, a whole new attitude to life, and a set of priorities which have been turned on their head.

Sometimes we can't cope with such stark reminders of our own mortality. And because *we* haven't come to terms with the possibility of death, we think the person suffering hasn't either. So we pretend that everything is as it was. That's not helpful.

Let's be positive. One out of two cancer patients will be alive, disease free, five or more years from this day. For some forms of cancer the cure rate is as high as nine out of ten.

Emotional attitudes have a powerful influence on the body's immune and restorative powers. Positive thinking won't cure cancer, but it sure does help.

Good positive emotions like hope, faith, love, laughter and a will to live, do have a curative effect on the body.

6 May

Is it a Stroke?

Sometimes symptoms of a stroke are difficult to identify. Unfortunately, the lack of awareness spells disaster for the stroke victim. A stroke victim may suffer brain damage when people nearby fail to recognise the symptoms of a stroke. Now doctors say any bystander can recognise a stroke by asking three simple questions:

* Ask the individual to smile.
* Ask him or her to raise both arms.
* Ask the person to speak a simple sentence.

If he or she has trouble with any of these tasks, call emergency service immediately and describe the symptoms to the operator.

7 May

Cancer II
Those who work constantly with cancer patients recognise typically unhelpful types:

- First there's the cheer leader, 'We can lick this thing, you'll be right as rain in no time.'
- There's overprotection: 'Whatever you do, you're not to lift that vacuum cleaner. Just lie down and rest.'
- Equally disconcerting is the opposite, which ignores the sickness. 'Shall we plan a mountain-climbing holiday just after Christmas?'
- Then there's the temptation to chat incessantly. The patient might want nothing more than someone to sit with. Let the patient control your help.

Even the most highly trained make mistakes. I know – I have been trying to learn the art of journeying with the sick for more than 30 years now. I still feel utterly inadequate.

The person who has cancer feels isolated and, incredible as it seems, there are still people who behave as if cancer is contagious. So it's important to visit, to sit close, to touch, to hug, to be comforting and reassuring.

Be sensitive to how the patient is at this particular time of this particular day. A patient may be bright and chatty in the morning and be dead beat at lunch time. Because patients become actors, they often behave in the way they think you want them to behave. You need to give them permission to be themselves.

8 May

Face Up runs articles on fame and fab advice on how to bust exam stress. For example, you should get plenty of sleep. Staying refreshed keeps everything in perspective. Take time to chill out. Find the best way of relaxing that suits you whether it be a long bath, listening to music or going for a walk.

If you are relaxed you won't panic. If you want to keep your stamina going, have a healthy diet. Take plenty of fruit and veg which will give you energy. Avoid artificial stimulants like tea and fizzy drinks which not only hype you up but dull your thinking.

9 May

How to survive a heart attack when alone
Since many people are alone when they suffer a heart attack, without help, the person whose heart is beating improperly and who begins to feel faint, has only about 10 seconds left before losing consciousness. However, these victims can help themselves by coughing repeatedly and very vigorously. A deep breath should be taken before each cough, and the cough must be deep and prolonged, as when producing sputum from deep inside the chest.

A breath and a cough must be repeated about every two seconds without let-up until help arrives, or until the heart is felt to be beating normally again. Deep breaths get oxygen into the lungs and coughing movements squeeze the heart and keep the blood circulating. The squeezing pressure on the heart also helps it regain normal rhythm.

10 May

The fact that people are put out of hospital because they are too old to cure, says more about the state of our medical system than it does about respect for the elderly. Since, by any standards, I am now more old age than middle age, I have an interest in this.

But consider where the top jobs are going these days. The Pope takes over 1.2 billion Catholics at the age of 78. The leader of the biggest party in Northern Ireland is Dr Ian Paisley, and he's in his 80th year. And the man who has taken on the most important job in the world, namely running Manchester United FC, is 68. I take great consolation from this. At least there are three important jobs in the world for which I am 20 years too young. That won't happen much longer. I'm enjoying it while I can.

11 May

My Lord God, I have no idea where I am going.
I do not see the road ahead of me.
I cannot know for certain where it will end.
Nor do I really know my own self,
and the fact that I think I am following your will does not necessarily mean that I am actually doing so.
But I believe that the desire to please you does in fact please you
and I hope I have that desire in everything that I do. I hope that I will never do anything apart from that desire. And I know that if I do this you will lead me by the right road even though I may know nothing about it. Therefore I will trust you always.
Even though I may seem to be lost and in the shadow of death I will fear no evil, for you are ever with me and you will never leave me to face my peril alone.
(Thomas Merton)

12 May

My favourite story about Adlai Stevenson relates to Norman Vincent Peale.

When, in the early 60s, Nixon and John F. Kennedy were running for office, there was a constant battle between the two sides. Many people were seriously concerned that Kennedy, being a Catholic, would be under the influence of the Vatican and that it would be bad for America. One of the people who argued this was Norman Vincent Peale. He even quoted from St Paul's writings which he claimed backed up his view that no member of the Roman Catholic Church should ever become President of America.

Adlai Stevenson was one of the people who was supporting Kennedy and when he was asked on television what he thought of Norman Vincent Peale's claim that it was written in the letters of St Paul that a Catholic could not become President of America, Stevenson thought for a moment and replied: 'I find Paul appealing, but Peale appalling.'

13 May

Remarkable obituary

Today we mourn the passing of a beloved old friend, Mr Common Sense. Mr Sense had been with us for many years.

He will be remembered as having cultivated such valuable lessons as knowing when to come in out of the rain, why the early bird gets the worm and that life isn't always fair. Common Sense lived by simple, sound financial policies (don't spend more than you earn) and reliable parenting strategies (adults, not kids, are in charge)

His health began to rapidly deteriorate when schools were required to get parental consent to administer aspirin to a student, but could not inform the parents when a student became pregnant and wanted to have an abortion.

Finally, Common Sense lost the will to live as the Ten Commandments became contraband; churches became businesses; and criminals received better treatment than their victims.

Common Sense was preceded in death by his parents, Truth and Trust, his wife, Discretion, his daughter, Responsibility, and his son, Reason. Two stepbrothers, My Rights and Ima Whiner, survive him.

Not many attended his funeral because so few realised he was gone.

14 May

'One of the most obvious characteristics of our daily lives is that we are busy. We experience our days as filled with things to do, people to meet, projects to finish, letters to write, calls to make and appointments to keep ... There are always people we did not speak to or write to or visit, so while we are very busy we have a lingering feeling of never really fulfilling our obligations.

'Beneath our worrying lives, however, there is something else going on. While our hearts and minds are filled with many things and we wonder how we can live up to the expectations imposed on us by ourselves and others, we have a deep sense of unfulfillment. The great paradox of our time is that we are busy and bored at the same time. ... In short, while our lives are full, we are unfulfilled.' (Thought from *Making all Things New* by Fr Henri Nouwen.)

15 May

I tried to read Dan Brown's book, *The Da Vinci Code,* a number of times. Each time after 20 or 30 pages, I realise I should be doing something more worthwhile – like reading the Bible where I would find the true portrait of Jesus and Mary Magdalene.

Personally, I don't believe that Jesus was married to Mary Magdalene. But even if he were, what huge difference would it make to belief? What would be so wrong with the Word made flesh being married? Let me repeat, I don't believe he was. But to shout too loudly that he couldn't have been or that it would have made him a less a Saviour, indicates an unhealthy view of sex in general and women in particular.

What frightened me was that a survey carried out in England found that three out of five people think there is some truth in the Code's theory that Jesus was married and had children by Mary Magdalene. That shows how gullible many are. Even more importantly, it shows how lacking in knowledge the vast majority of people are about the Bible.

16 May

Face Up is a terrific magazine which I look forward to each month. Here are their Seven Commandments of Celebrity Watching (or how to stay grounded while you gobble up the gossip). Know that:
1. Being rich and famous comes at a price – their lives are not always as great as they seem.
2. Being stick thin is neither normal nor healthy – not to be imitated.
3. The cult of celebrity is all about how things look – often at the expense of integrity, modesty and kindness.
4. Many celebs are vain and insecure, not qualities we would want for ourselves.
5. Celebs, like others, may be shy deep down. But they can't escape the spotlight and may use alcohol and drugs to mask those feelings.
6. Celebrities can be badly hurt by gossip about their private lives. What's a fun read for us, may be causing real pain to real people.
7. Thinking you look ugly in comparison to a celeb is a false exercise – without their makeup on and clothes picked out by their stylist, they often look very different.

17 May

One of the most magnificent things Pope John XXIII did when he became Pope was to visit a jail in Rome two days after Christmas. It was called *Regina Coeli,* which means Queen of Heaven. A terrible name for a prison. When he arrived at the prison, to the shock of everybody, he spoke to them: 'Since you could not come to see me, I have come to see you.' That's what it means to descend into other people's hells to help them.

He told them he came from a poor background. In Italy he said there are three ways to lose money: gambling, women and drink, and farming. And he added, 'Unfortunately, my father chose the least interesting way to be poor.' He also said that his brother had done time in prison for poaching fish. So he said, 'We are all children of God and I am your brother.'

On the same day a murderer in the prison came to him and said, 'Can even I be forgiven?' John said nothing to him, but hugged him and that picture went around the world. And the hug said everything. The hug, in fact, took him out of his hell.

18 May

Khrushchev's daughter Rada and her husband were received in the Vatican by Pope John XXIII. He asked her to name her children. 'I know the names of your children already, but there's nothing as beautiful as hearing a mother saying the names of her own children.' He said, 'Give them all a hug from me, especially Ivan,' which is the Russian for John.

When they were leaving he gave her Rosary beads. 'I know you don't believe in the Rosary, but I want to give you a peaceful memory. And the most peaceful memory I have is of my mother kneeling by the fireside saying the Rosary. And that's the peaceful feeling I want to give to you as a mother.'

Finally, he wanted to give his blessing to her. And his blessing was given not as the blessing of a Pope because they wouldn't accept that, 'but I know you will accept the blessing of an old peasant man.' And they did.

19 May

There was a famous man called Metropolitan Anthony Bloom who was for many years the head of the Russian Orthodox Church in Great Britain. He was an authority on prayer. But towards the end of his life he wrote an article in which he admitted that his prayer was becoming more and more superstitious. He had the mistaken idea that if he gave God enough attention, God would look after him.

He was helped by a trusted priest who gave him unusual advice. He told him to stop praying for a month except for this simple exercise. 'Before you go to bed at night say five times, "May the prayers of those who love me, save me". Then to bed and think of all those people who love you. And when a face or name comes to your mind, thank God for their love.'

Before long Anthony discovered a valuable truth – that all prayer is gratitude. Gratitude for the love of God and for the love of others in our lives.

20 May

A little girl told her father that her brothers were setting traps to catch birds. She was very upset. So he asked her what she was going to do about it. She said, 'I pray that the traps will not work and the birds will go free.'

'Anything else?' her father asked.

'I pray that God will direct the birds away from the trap,' she answered.

'And is that all you did?' the father teased.

She said, 'When the boys weren't looking, I kicked the traps into the ditch.'

Now there's a little girl who understood prayer. 'God helps those who help themselves.'

I love the prayer used by St Thomas More: 'O God, give me the grace to work for the things I pray for.' Which brings us back to the little girl kicking the traps into the ditch.

21 May

A Lifetime
It takes a lifetime to learn to live
How to share and how to give
How to face tragedy that comes your way
How to find courage to face each new day
How to smile when your heart is sore
How to go on when you can take no more
How to laugh when you want to cry
How to be brave when you say goodbye
How to love when your loss is great
How to forgive when you want to hate
How to be sure that God's really there
How to find him – seek him in prayer.
(Anon)

22 May

As one who is from the North and who has lived for the last 20 years here, there were many days when I gave in to despair about our future. Yet there was always a little glimmer of hope in the goodness of people both Protestants and Catholics. So encourage goodness wherever you find it.

One book which every house should have is *Lost Lives*. It the tragic story of every single person, almost 4,000 of them, who lost their lives in the North. That book should be a constant reminder of the futility of war. And when the Northern Assembly finds the going difficult, as it inevitably will, take out *Lost Lives* to realise what the alternative to peace is.

23 May

Anyone who doubts where innocent children go when they die hasn't even begun to understand our loving God. Theologians who have argued the existence of limbo for centuries made God into a tyrant beyond respect and impossible to believe in.

Innocent children go straight to heaven to enjoy eternal happiness with the God who created them in love. For reasonable and normal human beings, that is self-evident.

If theologians can't make that simple fact fit their system, then their system is wrong and they should be humble enough to admit it.

Instead they invented ridiculous theories like limbo where children 'enjoyed' a state of natural happiness but could never be 'in communion with God'. Typical of those who live in their heads. They justified their untenable position by claiming it was an advance on St Augustine's fourth-century heretical position that unbaptised children went to hell. Big deal, I hear you say.

24 May

'I don't think I need to beg God's forgiveness for making love,' a married woman said, 'I don't carry around a lot of guilt regarding sexual experiences I have had because I believe we have made responsible decisions about intimacy and love in our own life.'

The basis of her view is that sex between two committed caring adults is an expression of love. It's an integral part of a sharing, loving relationship.

So how's the church going to make responsible people like that feel at home?

If you want a grown up church you have to start treating people like grown ups and stop treating them like immature brats.

The church has the right and the duty to teach clearly and compassionately about sex, sexuality, marriage and morality in general. But these days people will come to their own responsible conclusions about the use of their own sexuality and their own bodies. So what we say better be real and reasonable.

25 May

'To vote is not just a civic duty, but a serious moral responsibility and how we vote affects the welfare of our fellow citizens. History shows that when evil occurs it is only too often because good people did nothing to prevent it.' So says moral theologian Fr Seán Fagan SM. In other words, we get the politicians and the governments we deserve.

I also agree with him when he says that be-littling politicians is a serious error. Politics is an honourable vocation and the vast majority of politicians make great personal sacrifices.

'There is no such thing as "neutral politics". Politics is about the common good and this requires dialogue and tolerance when all sides must be heard without any exclusion,' Fr Fagan writes.

26 May

The hierarchy of England and Wales brought out a special letter in 1996 on the subject of politics and voting. They strongly warn people against voting for a single issue candidate (eg: Pro-Life, Anti-Gay). The elector needs to be confident that the person he or she is voting for is the best qualified of those offering themselves for election, one who can be trusted to legislate responsibly on behalf of the electorate on all matters before the government, including some that people are not yet aware of.

27 May

I'm sure most of you will remember when bishops used to ask the young people going for Confirmation some very hard questions. One day he was examining a class and he asked them, 'What must we do to get to heaven?' Nobody seemed to say very much. So he began to prompt them.

'Supposing a person sold their house, car and gave all their money to charity, would that get them to heaven?' The class answered no.

'Supposing someone left their job and went to work in the Foreign Missions for nothing for ten years. Would that get them to heaven?' Again the class answered no. He had another go at it: 'Supposing someone was very good to their children, husband, wife, their neighbours and even animals, would that get them to heaven?' Again the children answered no.

The bishop was getting a little frustrated at this time so he asked them, 'Well what must you do to get to heaven?' and one wee fellow shot up his hand and said, 'To get to heaven you've got to die first.'

28 May

Early one morning I was blessing boats at Innisclare near the Manor House. There were about 50 boats to be blessed and there was a gathering of around 60 people on the shore. The rain had ceased and there was a very bright and beautiful sun. It was warm too. As I stood on the shore blessing the boats, I was looking out on all the green islands in Lough Erne. It was a heavenly scene. I realised that for hundreds and hundreds of years people had come from all over the world to pray on those very islands. They stopped off for peace and quiet in Cleenish, Devenish, Inishmacsaint and many others. I thought that if you couldn't find God in Lough Erne, you would have difficulty finding him anywhere.

As I drove back a thought struck me: The Eucharist that I was about to celebrate here in The Graan was the very same Eucharist that was celebrated on those islands for probably for 1500 years. People for all that time had gathered round altars in little churches in little islands and found food for their journey through life.

29 May

I was pleasantly surprised to read a quotation from St Augustine. He said it a long long time ago – about fifteen hundred years in fact. And he said, 'Don't ever send your children to school so that they can learn what the teacher thinks. Children go to school to learn to think for themselves.' It's worth contemplating.

I presume he would have given the same advice about preaching. You don't come to church to be told what to think by a preacher. At least I hope you don't. Our job as preachers is to offer the full challenge of the gospel in a way that not only allows but encourages each hearer, including myself, to make up our individual minds as to how we follow Christ and live out those challenges.

30 May

I was down at a wedding in Clare. One of the girls getting married was a solicitor. And as you know, I have great time for lawyers but very little time for law. So I thought of a little story about a couple who were going out together and sadly were killed and went to heaven. Peter let them into heaven, which means you can get into heaven even though you are *not* married. When they got to heaven they kept pestering Peter to get married. Peter said, 'You don't need to get married. This is heaven. You are supposed to be happy here.' But they kept pestering him. After about 100 years he called them aside one day and said, 'OK. I have the priest ready. You can get married now.' Which they did. And the marriage lasted about 30 years and then they started looking for a divorce. So they went to Peter and said, 'Could we get a divorce?' Peter said, 'Well it has taken me a 100 years to get a priest into heaven. How long do you think it's going to take me to get lawyer into heaven to get you a divorce?'

31 May

There was a priest who was changed to a parish near Las Vegas. He was full of brilliant ideas and began to learn how to sell his products, by looking at how they did it on The Strip. He was very successful and the crowds began to come. This aroused the interest of the bishop who came to visit him. He stayed a few days and he was impressed by some of the things his priest did. He called him aside and he explained to him that the drive-through confessionals he had started was a terrific idea. He was also very impressed by this new twenty-four service he was offering as it helped a lot of people who did shifts to be able to come. 'But,' said the bishop, 'I have to draw a line at this flashing neon sign which says TOOT AND TELL OR GO TO HELL. That simply is too far and it has got to go.'

1 June

Once in *The New York Times* a young father wrote an editorial to mark Father's Day. The ten tips he offered to parents, and especially to fathers who take an active part in rearing their children, were important:

1. It is impossible to raise a hang-up free child. Wanting perfect children is a hang-up in itself.
2. The way my children speak to each other is an accurate reflection of the way my wife and I are speaking to each other. Children are both sponges and mirrors.
3. Holding my children accountable for their own choices and decisions gives them the best shot at maturity.
4. Every criticism I give must be balanced at some point by a sign of acceptance and praise. Child abuse is only sometimes physical.
5. My children need my time, a lot of it – reading a story, fixing a broken truck, playing games – are all of more value than working a sixty hour week for things they do not really need.
6. There can never be too much laughter or music in a home.
7. Touching is more important than talking.
8. The child who drives me crazy making himself unlovable, is the child who needs my love the most.
9. If a child is without grandparents, serious consideration should be given to adopting some. Life's bumpy road with mum and dad calls for a good pair of shock absorbers.
10. I must try not to be afraid or ashamed to ask for help when my own resources as a father fail me.

2 June

When Cardinal Ratzinger was elected Pope and took the name Benedict XVI it's fair to say that there were many who were disappointed. Personally, I wasn't greatly enthused but it was obvious for the last five years who the next Pope was going to be.

Since his election I have been asked repeatedly by people on the street, what I think of the new Pope. My answer is the same to everyone. I believe in the Holy Spirit. I believe that despite human politics, God will look after his people and I always add, 'It's only fair to give the man a chance. Benedict XVI doesn't have to be the same as Cardinal Ratzinger.'

3 June

Just for Today: Part One
Just for today I will try to live through this day only, and not tackle all my problems at once. I can do something for twelve hours that would appal me if I felt I had to keep it up for a lifetime.

Just for today I will be happy. Most of us are as happy as we make up our minds to be.

Just for today, I will adjust myself to what is, and not try to adjust everything to my own desires. I will take my 'luck' as it comes, and fit myself to it.

Just for today I will try to strengthen my mind. I will study, I will learn something useful. I will read something that requires effort, thought and concentration.

4 June

Just for Today: Part Two
Just for today I will exercise my soul in three ways: I will do somebody a good turn and not get found out; if anybody knows of it, it will not count. I will do at least two things I don't want to do – just for exercise. I will not show anyone that my feelings are hurt; they may be hurt, but today I will not show it.

Just for today I will be agreeable. I will look as well as I can, dress becomingly, talk low, act courteously, criticise not one bit, not find fault with anything and not try to improve or regulate anybody but myself.

Just for today I will have a programme. I may not follow it exactly, but I will have it. I will save myself from two pests: hurry and indecision.

Just for today I will have a quiet half hour all by myself, and relax. I will try to get a better perspective on my life.

Just for today I will be unafraid. Especially I will not be afraid to enjoy what is beautiful, and to believe that as I give to the world, so the Father will give to me.

5 June

I have been telling anyone who will listen that in my mind there is a connection between cannabis abuse at a young age and the onset of mental disturbance a few years later.

That's why I was fascinated by a BBC *Panorama* programme on which Terry Hammond told about his son Steve. Terry strongly believes that Steve's cannabis abuse was one of the reasons why his son developed schizophrenia. Furthermore, he's convinced that had he not smoked cannabis he would not have developed the condition.

The programme was fair in that it did not accuse cannabis of being the cause of schizophrenia. Lots of people smoke cannabis and are completely free of any symptoms. They have no problem and enjoy it. But there are others who, because of their genes or some other predisposition, are more vulnerable to its effects.

The bottom line is that mood altering drugs are always a risk. People who respect their life, their future, and their gifts don't get involved. It's as simple as that.

6 June

There's a young man presently detained in Wheatfield Prison who writes to me regularly. He's a gifted writer. His most recent letter to me explained the sheer hell he is enduring as he is detoxed from methadone. He is a heroin addict who, through the work of the clinic in the prison, is now on methadone. He knows if he is to be a writer and use other talents in the arts, he'll have to come off methadone too.

'I don't desire the clinic life, living from one cup of Meth to the next one. It's one of my biggest fears,' he admits. 'I've put so much hard work into educating myself and breaking into the Arts world that I know I can be productive and contribute positively to society. I can make amends and even do some work with young offenders, sharing my strength, hope and experiences with them …'

In each letter, he writes passionately about the scandal of homelessness. In his case, when his sentence is completed, he's given a bus fare and a plastic bag. He has nowhere to go, no money and no support to help him stay off drugs. He knows within a short time he'll be back in prison.

7 June

If you want to be miserable, here are a few rules which never fail. They will certainly take the joy out of your life and probably destroy anyone you happen to meet along the way.

1. Feel sorry for yourself. It's a perfect place to start. Self pity is guaranteed to make you miserable.

2. Make a list of things that could go wrong but probably won't. Next start worrying about them. It's amazing what can go wrong if you start looking for trouble.

3. If you want to make your own and others' lives miserable you can do it with one single word. Complain. Find fault with everything. Eventually you will become an expert complainer. And when you do you will find flaws everywhere. Never mind the good points, just concentrate on the negative.

4. Insist on bullying other people so that you can always have your own way. Pretend to listen but don't. Don't co-operate. Don't compromise. Don't give in. And when things get tough, quit. You'll have enough misery to last you a lifetime.

5. Gossip and ridicule. Highlight other people's weaknesses. Tell them to their face how bad they are. Talk behind their backs too. You'll spread misery like a contagious disease.

6. Make a mountain out of a mole hill. Over react to everything. Emphasise what is worst in your workplace, your surroundings, your family, yourself and in the people you have to deal with. Accentuate the negative. Speak in an angry voice. You'll spread so much misery you could become too happy.

7. Be selfish and self-centred. Why be concerned about others? If asked to help say no. Even if not asked, develop the kind of face that says, 'Don't come near me.' Let someone else do it. Misery will be your constant companion.

8. Don't entertain compassion, forgiveness or understanding. You have much more important things to do. Open the door to such positive thoughts and your misery could disappear.

So don't mess with misery. If you do you could begin to laugh at yourself. And if you do your misery will crumble. Be warned.

8 June

John Mc Gahern says in *Amongst Women*, 'You can only love what you know.' He went on to say, 'The best journeys in life are always among the familiar.' I think that's wonderful. Essentially it means that our best journeys are not away to somewhere else, but among the familiar territory that we now know. Journeys inwards, in other words. How can we love ourselves if we don't even know ourselves? And how can we know ourselves if we don't reflect upon our lives? How can we love God if we don't know God? Which God is it that we know? I have spent a lot of my life with people who say they don't believe in God anymore. And when you ask them which God they don't believe in, I discover I couldn't believe in it either. They don't believe in the vengeful, frightening, fearsome God of their youth and of their catechism. They haven't made the journey inward. They haven't reflected upon God. The best journeys are among the familiar and that's when we learn to love and to know ourselves and God.

9 June

Kelly Holmes was a British hero at the Athens Olympics when she won double gold. She was a beautiful, strong, athletic, trim, happy, successful woman without a care in the world. It was quite a shock then to learn that less than a year before the Olympics she was on the point of suicide, and had repeatedly cut her wrists with scissors. It was serious self harm and in different circumstances could have been fatal.

Self harm is a growing phenomenon, especially amongst women. Those in most danger are perfectionists who set themselves high goals and who are so used to achieving those goals that failure is an unwanted and destructive experience. They put pressure on themselves.

Psychologists say that self harming is a way for them to feel that they are still in control. The pain is a release. It is the equivalent of bursting into tears.

Happily, Kelly has shown it can be overcome and, since her gold medal achievement, life has been good for her.

10 June

I was reading recently the true story of Major James Nesmeth. He wanted to improve his golf game. The first time he set foot on a golf course after his seven-year lay off, he shot an astonishing 74. That was 20 strokes better than his previous best.

Major Nesmeth had in fact spent those seven years as a prisoner of war in North Vietnam. During that time he was imprisoned in a cage, four and a half feet high and five feet long. During the time he was imprisoned he saw no one, talked to no one, experienced no physical contact with anyone else. So he realised he needed to occupy his mind or he'd lose his sanity. He learned to focus and visualise.

In his mind he had a vision of a splendid golf course and began playing 18 holes of golf every day in his mind. He imagined every last detail. In his mind he was actually on the course. It took him just as long to play the course in his mind as it would in reality. Seven days a week, four hours a day, eighteen holes, for seven years. That's how he took twenty shots off his game.

I really don't need to mention that if we developed the same ability to focus and imagine in other areas of our lives, we would improve just as much as the Major did.

11 June

We can be very proud of U2 and what they do for Ireland. Bono is one of the leading spokespersons in the world on behalf of the poor. Not everybody agrees with his tactics, nor with his reasoning. But then it's much easier to criticise than it is to be positive. If all of the rest of us used our voices as effectively as Bono does, then not only world poverty but also poverty on the streets of Ireland would be eliminated.

Generally, we in Ireland have a despicable habit of dismissing those who prod at our consciences. We make excuses for well-known Irish people who make fools of themselves in Hollywood and other places. But we attribute the worst possible motives to people like Geldoff, Bono and Daniel O Donnell who each in turn have made a magnificent contribution to the poor and deprived in every corner of the world. You too can support U2. Be proud of their achievements. Well done, Bono and the boys.

12 June

At least Dan Brown's *Da Vinci Code* is clearly labelled as a novel. Some of the foolishness portrayed about the film by Catholic groups is more insidious and dangerous, because it claims to be factual. It isn't. It's nonsense.

One ray of hope though is that the *Catholic Digest*, an American magazine not known for its liberal views, just released the result of a poll about *The Da Vinci Code*. It found that 73% of Catholics who read the book said it did not reflect on their faith or opinion of the church. The editor in-chief, Dan Connors, said as a result of the poll, 'On the whole, Catholics see fiction for what it is – fiction.' Hope springs eternal.

13 June

'I love the people I run into, but I pity them for having to live as they do. And I think, the world of the US is a world of crass, blind, overstimulated, phoney, lying stupidity. The war gets slowly worse – and almost more inane. The temper of the country is one of blindness, fat, self-satisfied, ruthless, mindless corruption. All of the best people are uneasy about it and helpless to do anything against it. The rest are perfectly content with the rat-race as it is, and with its competitive, acquisitive, hurtling, souped-up drive into nowhere. A massively aimless, baseless, cockiness that simply exhausts itself without purpose. The mindless orgasm, in which there is no satisfaction, only spasm.'

A fine piece of modern writing? Not at all. It's a fine piece of writing from exactly 40 years ago.

The person who wrote it is even more surprising. It was written by Fr Thomas Merton who died in 1968. He was the foremost spiritual writer of the 20th century.

The question that we may be afraid to face though is this: Is his description of America 40 years ago a pretty accurate insight into the Ireland of today?

14 June

Vincent Van Gogh said that God always sends us works of art so that we can see ourselves in them, and he went on to say that, 'The greatest artist of all is Christ who doesn't work with canvas but rather with human flesh.'

Now there's a lovely thought – even if my life is a failure, I am still one of God's great works of art.

15 June

The death of Charles J. Haughey was not unexpected. I'm glad he got a state funeral, because the word 'disgraced' is a cruel way to remember any man who held office and who did, 'some good for the state'. I am not enamoured with our new morality which is unforgiving and selective.

It is also important to remember his family. I have met all of them and know some of them quite well. His wife Maureen is a lady who maintained her dignity through many trials and tribulations. Sean also had to endure more than his fair share of begrudgery. He, too, has always behaved with the kind of dignity and decorum which only comes with class and character.

Charlie himself, as everybody knows, was an enigma. I met him on many occasions. During his most difficult times, I frequently shared a meal with him in a mutual friend's house. I found him to be highly entertaining but sometimes shifty. He was, however, a consummate survivor with a far more brilliant mind than he was given credit for.

He most certainly helped to shape for better or worse, the kind of Ireland and the kind prosperity we now have. Nobody is all good, but nobody is all bad either, and it is good to forgive the bad and be grateful for the many good things he left us.

16 June

The Catholic Church in Ireland today is in crisis and, contrary to what many in my profession think, it's no solution to hope for things to return to how they were.

Some say it's too late for the church in Ireland; that the church is dead. I hope the church as we know now will soon be gone forever, but there is hope. Church attendances may have dropped significantly but the number of people still declaring themselves Catholic has barely altered. That tells me people need some religion, that a basic faith is part of the Irish psyche. It is our duty as priests to figure out what direction we need to take our church in, in order to restore trust in the Catholic Church.

17 June

From the several thousand letters a year I receive, it is obvious most people think the present church structures and strictures are at best irrelevant. I agree with them. It will take courage and leadership to deal with these problems. Some of the unmentionables we should be discussing are:

- Our preaching is out of date.
- Priests don't have to be single and celibate. If some want it that way, let them choose it but don't confine the gift of priesthood to single males with an imposed vow of celibacy.
- Listen to the people. Give them real power. Trust them with money. Trust their commitment.
- Welcome women to genuine leadership roles.
- Learn a new sexual morality from married people. At present, no matter what we say, we really do believe that sex is bad. Look at the damage we've done to ourselves and others living out this falsehood. Sex is good and a gift from God.
- Let the laity have a say in who they want as their priest/leader and let both priests and laity choose their bishop.

18 June

How do you keep so happy all the time? Your laugh is completely heart-warming. *Helen in Cork.*

Reply: Thanks Helen. I'm, glad you like it. It's also, according to many others, my most annoying trait. I get more complaints about my laugh than I do about what I say. As far as I am concerned it's the way I feel. I'm very easy to make laugh. Brendan Grace, the comedian, used to say that he'd love to take me around all his shows because no matter how many times I see his show he can always hear my laugh from the audience. I take that as a compliment.

There are days when I don't laugh all that easily because like everybody else I let pressure get to me. So any day I get a chance to laugh, I roar my head off and it's totally natural. I can cry just as easily though. I'm an emotional person, thank God.

19 June

We need faith and we need some way to express it in religious rituals. We need a higher power. Even now, in a time when people have stopped going to church, they get into séances, black magic, gurus – all of these things are a replacement for religion.

There is something in the human psyche that needs religion. We need ways of understanding the world. We need reasons for living. We need to understand what the point of our existence is.

The French existentialist philosopher, Teilhard de Chardin, once said: 'We are not human beings on a spiritual journey, we are spiritual beings on a human journey.'

We are always searching, reaching. The heart doesn't rest.

20 June

Thank you for always being so nice to gay people. I'm gay and find it very hard when the church says I'm a bad person – why can't they all be like you? *Con in Cork.*

Reply: Thank you, Con. I'm delighted you take some courage from what I say. Don't ask me to explain why other priests, and indeed many other people in society, have such a fear and a hatred of people who are gay. It's against anything Christ would want. In fact, I would find it difficult to respect anything those who are cruel to gay people would say on any other topic. Perhaps they haven't come to terms with their own sexuality and what they resent is what they fear most.

As far as I am concerned, God makes each of us special and loves each of us exactly as we are. God does not deal in second hand goods. God makes everybody good. It is absolutely ludicrous that God would make anyone's sexuality a source of punishment. Sexuality is the greatest gift God gives us and it needs to be respected for that reason. Sexuality is always meant to be an expression of a loving concern for ourselves and others. God loves everyone, whatever their sexuality. And that's why I try to respect those who are gay from a deep sense of conviction. That's where I come from, but I can't comment on where those who are anti-gay come from. They are pretty arrogant when doing it for themselves.

21 June

The church can never again hold the same position it did in Ireland 20 years ago. But we need religion, because without it, life is meaningless. The only positive choice the church can take is to reform radically from being a clerical church to being, from the roots up, a people of God community. We need another reformation.

The deeply ingrained evil of clericalism is destroying the credibility of our beautiful church. Because of it, one essential point has been missed and no amount of rearranging the deck chairs will camouflage it. The point is this: The church will be saved by its laity, or it will not be saved at all.

22 June

Every week I get letters from distraught parents, who are at their wits' end because of their children's alcohol abuse. Invariably they conclude the letter by saying, 'I suppose it could be worse – they could be on drugs.' And that's their first mistake. Alcohol *is* a legalised drug – potentially good, but lethal in the wrong hands.

And alcohol abuse is not confined to young people. It's just as obvious in the over fifties as it is in the under twenties. Again we all know that alcohol abuse by women is on the increase. We Irish don't appear to handle alcohol well, even on social occasions. A recent study showed that out of every ten drinking sessions, six ended in binge drinking. Every sad event, every happy event and every event in between is an occasion not only to enjoy a drink, but to drink to excess. That's the reality.

23 June

There has been a long list of clerics making futile statements condemning various Penitential Services and Liturgical Services which people find attractive and meaningful. Lay people know precisely what they would like to find when they come to church. They know that when people make reconciliation difficult, it has nothing to do with the spirituality of the gospels and everything to do with the abuse of human power. Anyone who prays the gospels knows that Jesus treated sinners in a merciful and loving way.

Every time I read the New Testament I marvel at how frequently Jesus tells us not to put limits on God's kingdom. There is no question of excluding. People who genuinely seek the truth will find God waiting for them. They will have a place in God's kingdom.

24 June

We need to encourage a mature attitude to both sin and life. I'm in the lucky position that I spend hours every week helping people in the Sacrament of Reconciliation. It's always a problem when people ramble through a list of sins which mean nothing to them, to God or to me. It's wonderful when people come in for a chat and find peace in the story of their own lives and their own brokenness.

Irish people in general have a dreadful sense of their own self-worth. If anything, they judge themselves too harshly. My task is to help them find their gifts, their talents, their goodness and help them to be grateful for the grace they have received. From that position they don't need me or anyone else to tell them where they are failing or where they can improve.

25 June

God has to be the centre of the spiritual life. Responsibility and gratitude grow out of a recognition that we owe everything to the God of love. If I really want to know God, I read the gospels. Two stories stand out. In the story of the Prodigal Son the sinner (the son) prepared his list well, but God (the father) didn't want to listen to it. He was looking out for his return, saw he was genuine, wrapped his arms around him, forgave him, and ordered a party to celebrate his return. That's the truth.

The second story I remember is the time our first Pope, St Peter, sinned by denying Jesus. He was treated with respect, not scorn. Jesus didn't force him or the other vulnerable disciples to crawl. He asked one question only: 'Do you love me?' In the end that's all that matters.

26 June

St Francis was a reluctant saint. But eventually he decided that he wanted to help the poor. One day he was going along the road and he met a leper. What he *should* have done was walk in the opposite direction and have nothing to do with the leper. What *in fact* he did was cross the road and kissed the leper. That changed his life. He crossed the chasm of fear at that point.

Later he said it wasn't the physical act of crossing the road and kissing the leper which was most important, but it was confronting the leper/rottenness within himself, acknowledging it and loving it. He recognised that there was both good and bad within himself. And he was happy with the good and bad within himself. That's what gave him the strength to do great things with his life afterwards.

It's a good lesson for each of us. Look into our own lives, recognise the gifts God has given us; also recognise the dark side of our life. Come to terms with that dark side, cross the chasm of fear and use the gifts that God has given us. It sounds simple but it is very difficult.

27 June

Two old Dublin ladies were talking about saints. One of them leaned across the fence and said, 'Mary, you know my husband is a pure saint.' To which Mary replied, 'Well Bridget you are lucky, cause mine is still alive.'

I suppose that's what makes a saint anyway. You have to be dead first.

28 June

A Parent's Confession
For that smile I didn't give you, I am sorry;
For that afternoon I didn't spend with you, I am sorry;
For that story I didn't have time to listen to, I am sorry;
For all the times I should have said, 'Well done' and didn't, I am sorry;
For the hug I didn't return to you, I am sorry;
For that joke I didn't laugh at, I am sorry;
For every time I didn't have time, I am sorry;
For having belittled you in front of your friends, I am sorry;
For having demanded your love instead of earning it with kindness, laughter, a Godly example, I am sorry;
For every instance when I've taken you for granted rather than recognise you as an individual person with your own particular dreams and aspirations, I am sorry;
For understanding my errors and my desire to change, for your great love, for respect and forgiveness, I am thankful.
(Edited from St Columba's Newsletter)

29 June

John Newton worked on a ship carrying slaves from Africa to America. And he became such a successful slave trader that in his early twenties he was captain of this ship and a very wealthy man.

But a storm of life made him think again. He was coming with a shipload of slaves when off the coast of Donegal a huge storm blew up and they were shipwrecked. And he cried out to God, 'Lord if you save me I will become your slave forever.' And in the unjust way things happen, many of the slaves drowned and a rascal like John Newton was saved.

However he was true to his word and eventually he converted to Christianity, stopped slave trading, and studied for the ministry and was ordained an Anglican minister and served out a very good and pious life in Olney in England.

He devoted his life to preaching and to writing hymns. And one of the lovely hymns he wrote was the story of his life, *Amazing Grace*: 'Amazing grace how sweet the sound/that saved a wretch like me/ I once was lost but now I'm found/ was blind but now I see.'

30 June

A woman came to a priest one day to say that she had bought two parrots. They were two lady parrots. They were recommended as being top class talking parrots. But when she got them home and put them in a cage all the two parrots would say is, 'We're two loose ladies, do you want a good time?' And this after a week annoyed her intensely. So she sought the advice of the priest. What should she do? Would he come down and bless them?

The priest thought of the two parrots he himself had bought. They were two male parrots, called Moses and Jacob, and he had trained them well. They could pray, they could quote the Bible, they could even sing a hymn given the right birdseed. His suggestion was simple. His parrots couldn't go to her house in case they would be brought down to the level of the two ladies so the two ladies would have to come to his house. In no time at all they would join the men in praying, reading the Bible and singing hymns.

The woman brought her two parrots to the house and when she entered Moses and Jacob were in their cages saying The Rosary. The two ladies parrots were put in a cage and right enough they were as friendly as ever. The first thing they said was, 'Hi, we're two loose ladies, do you want a good time?' At that Jacob looked over at Moses and said, 'Moses, you can drop the Rosary beads, our prayers have been answered.'

1 July

A rare thing happened me this week. A bishop said and did something inspiring, Christ-like and truly heroic. The Bishop of Memphis Tennessee, Bishop Terry Steib, began his column in the *Diocesan Newspaper* by describing the church as a home where, 'Family gathers to celebrate God's unconditional love.' He went on to point out where, in his opinion, the church fails to be a home. 'I have become more acutely aware of the number of Catholics who are no longer comfortable in their home. In fact some are no longer certain that the church is their home.'

'How deep is our river of faith,' he asked, 'if we are not actively working to be sure that all are welcome in their own home – the home given to each of us when we became members of God's family through baptism? ... Will we allow our hearts to grow if we simply lay aside preconceived notions of who does or does not belong? ... Jesus loved all, lived for all, and died for all.'

2 July

The story is told about the former Secretary of State, Henry Kissinger, and the man he chose to be his biographer. He spent many days with the author and asked him to go away and write a draft for Kissinger's approval.

Months afterwards, the author submitted his first draft. He left it with Kissinger and after three days the former politician rang and asked him, 'Is this the best you can do?' The biographer replied, 'Henry, I thought so, but if you say so I'll try again.' So back he went to rewrite his work. He returned three weeks later with another draft. Incredibly, this same exchange went on eight times. After each of the eight drafts Kissinger asked the same question, 'Is this the best you can do?' Finally, the author submitted his ninth draft and was called into Kissinger's office two days later. Again Kissinger asked the same question. Exasperated, the author replied, 'Henry, I've beaten my brains out. This is the ninth draft. I know it's the best I can do. By this stage I couldn't possibly improve on one word of it.'

Kissinger then looked at his biographer and said, 'In that case, I will now read it.'

3 July

I was reading the letters of an old bishop who spent most of his working life working in secret. In China you cannot hurry from house to house no matter how limited your time is. You have to take things easy or at least appear to do so and you will find that in the evening you will have accomplished far more than the man who hurried and blustered all day long.

If a Chinese person happens to come in while you are taking your dinner he salutes you with 'eat easy'. If he meets you on the road it is 'walk easy'. If you are studying he tells you 'study easy'.

In China, things move more along in slow and easy stages and if you want to keep in line you too must take things easy.

As the old rhyme puts it:
What is this life, if full of care we have no time to stand and stare.
No time to stand beneath the boughs and stare as long as sheep or cows.
A poor life this if, full of care, we have no time to stand and stare.

4 July

No Moving Parts, No Batteries (or The Hug!)
No moving parts, no batteries.
No monthly payments and no fees;
Inflation proof, non-taxable,
In fact, it's quite relaxable;
It can't be stolen, won't pollute,
One size fits all, do not dilute.
It uses little energy,
But yields results enormously.
Relieves your tension and your stress,
Invigorates your happiness;
Combats depression, makes you beam,
And elevates your self esteem!
Your circulation it corrects – without unpleasant side effects

It is, I think, the perfect drug:
May I prescribe, my friend … the hug!
(and of course, fully returnable!) *(Author unknown)*

5 July

Recently I got a thank you card from children in a 'Special' school. On it was the prayer of St Francis. It brought me peace and I hope you can experience it too: 'Lord make me an instrument of your peace. Where there is hatred, let me sow love ... Where there is injury pardon ... Where there is doubt, faith ... Where there is darkness, light, and where there is sadness, joy ... For it is in pardoning that we are pardoned and it is in dying that we are born to eternal life.'

6 July

As I watched the unfolding chaos on 7/7 in London, it was the silence which got to me. Only a gigantic force could crush the life out of London and silence its many voices. And that's what happened. An evil power sucked life and wonder out of a city rightly celebrating the coming of the Olympic ideal. An ideal which cherishes everyone, which respects participation and applauds the universal values of life, happiness and achievement.

Respectful silence is a good first response to cowardly killers. It teaches us many lessons. It allows us to come to terms with the awful sickening grief any normal human being must feel. In silence the natural anger is acknowledged, not denied, and hopefully quelled just a little.

In silence there might even be time to listen to a loving God helping us find the stepping stones of consolation in this meaningless mess. Silence, even an eerie silence, helps us keep our dignity and our sanity.

7 July

Richard Rohr wrote: 'Once after I gave a retreat in Ireland, three older women came up and said, "Father, what you are saying is what we believed years ago, but we threw it out with the Second Vatican Council." They told me about the fallen priest. He was the priest who had some terrible moral failure, as if all of us didn't. The fallen priest was, of course, looked down upon and whisked away to some monastery on the coast of Ireland so the good Irish people wouldn't imagine that their priest sinned or drank. Yet the three women told me excitedly: "You know what? We don't know if the other priests knew this, but we always went to the fallen ones for the cure".'

8 July

One of the loveliest things to happen in *Live 8* was when Birhan Woldu from Ethiopia appeared on stage. She was a very pretty 24 year old who shared the stage with Madonna and Geldoff. She told the audience how she had been so close to death that her father actually wrapped her body in a burial shroud and waited for her to die. A picture was shown on screen, of an emaciated little girl with rotten teeth, dead eyes and flies on her wounds.

She had lost her mother and sister in the famine in Ethiopia but when aid workers found Birhan they were able to save her life. Now, 20 years later, she is a student of agriculture and able to tell the world that aid really does work. She's living proof of that fact.

9 July

The key word is forgiveness. We need to be able to accept who we really are and forgive ourselves for not being the perfect being we'd love to be. God has no trouble doing it. And it's time we learned that it is his love, not our painful endeavours, which helps us to grow slowly to what we can become.

Strangely when we're able to accept ourselves, we can accept others who aren't perfect more easily.

10 July

It is true that we can't reduce the gospel to a code of what we might call manageable rules for ourselves. Christ didn't come to destroy the Law but he did come to give us ideals which go far beyond laws and rules. 'Be compassionate as your Father is compassionate', was what Jesus said to us. We are pointed in the direction of very high principles. We may never attain them. We shouldn't be disillusioned when we don't. We should be humble enough to accept that we still have the journey to make. Eventually, through the grace of Christ, we'll get there.

11 July

Richard Rohr has a lovely take on the Prodigal Son's story. 'The father who Jesus knew looks amazingly like what most cultures would call mother ... the father is in every way the total opposite of the male patriarch and even rejects the older son's appeal to a world of worthiness and merit. He not only allows the younger son to make choices against him, but even empowers him to do so by giving him money ... Both his leaving and his returning are treated as necessary, but painful, acts of adult freedom.'

12 July

I was interested in the poll on Marian Finnucane's programme to chose the greatest Irish woman. The woman who won it was Nano Nagle. How many of you know Nano Nagle? She risked jail and indeed death to educate young children, particularly young Catholic girls. She was from Cork. She herself was educated at a hedge school and she gave up a privileged life in Paris when she opted to work with the poor. She founded her first school in a mud hut in 1752. She then went on to found the Presentation Sisters and eventually many other schools to educate young people. Her plan became the template for Catholic education everywhere.

13 July

I wonder what is it that stops us from being heroes? I believe our greatest crime is silence. You could add in begrudgery or jealously too.

Silence is the universal crime of decent people. We are silent in the face of evil because we don't want to get involved, are afraid of being snubbed, or of being rejected. But the silence of the many allows the malice of the few to triumph. It was the silence of the majority of Germans which allowed Hitler and his evil few to exterminate 6 million Jews. It was the silence of white Americans that allowed the murder of Martin Luther King. It was the silence of the vast majority of priests and bishops which allowed 5% of priests to wreck havoc on the church and, more evilly, destroy the lives of so many young children. Pilate washing hands is a good symbol of the cowardice which helps evil flourish.

14 July

When the second richest man in the world decides to give away most of his fortune to charity, then it is time for all of us to sit up. It's a shock to us, but can you imagine how his children must have felt? They were looking forward to the day when they would become super rich. Now they will have to make do with the crumbs from the rich man's table.

As I drive around Ireland now, I often feel that the newly rich display their wealth in a most vulgar way. There are too many ugly mansions popping up with gaudy electric gates and Las Vegas style flood lights springing out of the earth. They are destroying the countryside and enshrining vulgarity in wasteful follies.

You'd think they'd do something better with their wealth. For a country that despised the big house for most of its history, it's amazing to see the natives apeing the oppressor.

15 July

One of the things I like best in life is seeing children behaving like children. One of the awful things about modern society is that there is no time to be a child. The mature parents want their children to behave like grown-ups as soon as they are out of the cradle. Just go to a children's football match and listen to very silly parents damning their children for not being cynical cheats. Go to a dancing competition and be revolted by the way organisers and parents take the fun out of everything by dressing children up like gaudy Barbie dolls. Go to a first Holy Communion and see that not even a lovely spiritual day in the child's life is free of needless pretence.

16 July

Despite their parents' foolishness children at heart remain children. This is especially true when they get a chance to be free to talk to God in their own way. They cut through all the pious nonsense we so go on with and talk to God as if he were real. How odd?

Here are some examples from a class of ten-year-olds, misspellings and all:

'Dear Jesus, my sister is a teenager and she is always bossing me. Why couldn't you have made me be born sooner, then I would be a teenager now? Amen.'

'Lord, help me not to spoof. I hate telling fibs, so does everybody else. So kick Nick out. Amen.'

'Jesus, why do you put on all the good films at half ten when you know I am in bed?'

17 July

I am no expert on grieving, but here are a few suggestions about what not to do.

First of all, don't abandon those in need. A woman said to me recently that when her child was killed, people didn't know what to say, so they either said nothing or talked about everything else under the sun.

I never know when I am being helpful. I have to keep reading signs all the time and I know there are many times when I am not seen as being helpful, simply because I am not saying what the person wants to hear.

I have found that people often come back years later and tell me how I helped them, even though I was totally unaware of it at the time. Usually they say something like this: 'You allowed us to talk about it when we wanted to. You also allowed us to have all our feelings. You assured us we weren't going mad.'

Now how I did that, I don't know, but I am glad I did. I would say that's the core of how to be helpful.

18 July

It's just an ordinary tree, standing majestically in the valley of the field. From where I sit, I have the unusual experience of looking down on it. In spring it's dressed like a model. Leaves, each one different, make it rounded, full, symmetrical, but imperfect enough to be naturally beautiful.

A few weeks ago it was naked and skeletal. Six weeks on, the leaves will pale to a tired yellow, and then turn a sleepy brown before returning to a bony skeleton in October. The miracle is that it will be magnificent and beautiful in every season.

I've watched it for years now, giving food for thought and food to birds no matter how it looks. It gives me perspective in the troubles of life and priesthood and church. Life comes and life goes on – yours, mine and nature's. Each of us is a work of art, a canvass coloured uniquely by God, as he writes straight on crooked lines; imperfect enough to be beautiful and yet loved for what we are.

19 July

I was reading an American paper recently that the Dominican Order over there are celebrating 800 years of existence. That's a long time. There's a mountain of wisdom in 800 years of struggle. I love the question posed by the poet Sr Anne Willits to the conference. She asks: 'Are we coming or going?' What a wonderful question. What a difficult one to answer. The struggle to change in a healthy way goes on forever.

Struggles always begin with a shock. As the social reformer Saul Alinsky said, 'Change means movement. Movement means friction'.

We cannot sell out the future, simply because we want to hold on to the past. The secret is to try to understand that in the struggles of life we decide either to become new or simply to become older.

20 July

One Sunday morning a woman took a long walk and on her way back decided that she needed an ice-cream to cool her down.

She went into the only coffee/ice-cream shop open on Sunday. There was one other customer in the shop, and that was Paul Newman.

The woman went weak at the knees looking into those famous blue eyes. The actor nodded in a friendly way back to her and continued his coffee. She told herself to remember she was a middle-aged woman, happily married with three children and no longer a teenager.

The assistant took her order, and she took the ice-cream in one hand and her change in the other. When she went to her car she realised that she had a handful of change but no ice-cream. She went back into the store but there was no cone in sight. Paul Newman's face broke into that charming smile and with a friendly grin he said: 'You put it in your purse.' And she had. Blue eyes must be lethal.

21 July

The first time I met Denis Faul was in the early 70s. Denis had, for a number of years, been speaking out against injustices. It was unusual enough at the time and it was certainly not the way to curry favour with his immediate superiors, though it was a popular thing to do with the Nationalist people whom he served.

I remember asking him then why he put his head above the parapet so frequently and his answer was insightful. He told me his mother always taught him when he was a young boy that if a couple of decent German Christians had spoken out against Hitler they could have saved the lives of millions of Jews. If we don't speak out, then we are in a real way responsible for the crime.

It proves something I've realised for a long time – most of our best principles are given to us early in life, usually within our family. The rest of learning gives us a framework to work out what our mothers taught us.

22 July

I believe the church exists for humanity rather than to perpetuate its own existence. Sometimes we are so interested in saving the church that we have lost sight of saving the world. As Christians, we should not expect a detailed road map for the future. All we need to know is that there *is* a future. Christ promised to be with us always, to the end of time. We don't have to know every exact detail of where the future lies. We are on a journey of faith. If we get involved in church politics and have an infatuation with winning arguments, we will have a church trivial, small and worthless.

If, on the other hand, we can regain a passion for the gospel and the mystery of God's love, then the church will live again. We need to be able to seek truth, especially with those with whom we disagree. We need to see that the church has a tolerance for those who are different. In other words, if we have a passion for the gospel the church will look after itself.

23 July

There was some hope here in Ireland recently when it was shown that many people were moving away from ecstasy. It is quite plain now that our young people, particularly those in third level education, can't possibly achieve their proper academic results if they use ecstasy, or abuse drugs even in small doses.

In short, ecstasy is destroying the mental health of young people, frustrating their ability to achieve proper results, and building up massive problems with the early onset of alzheimers and possibly schizophrenia.

It doesn't take a genius to know that it is time we started talking hard facts to the young and old. The reality is that no more recreational drugs should be legalised. Those who claim there should be a tolerance of certain categories of drugs, simply don't know the facts. All drugs, it seems to me, when they are abused, do serious damage to our mental and physical health.

24 July

It's extraordinary that the more effort the Catholic Church in Ireland has put into Catholic education, the less Catholic have most of the pupils become. A serious review must be made of what we call Catholic education. I'm not speaking against it here, I'm merely asking for a debate on what it should be.

Surely a central part of it ought to be helping students to grow as spiritual people. I have nothing against Celtic tigers and the abolition of poverty, but we know it has a left a spiritual poverty in its wake. This is where the true gift of teaching is required. It will include adult religious education which is not just learning about what you can't do, but being imbued with the scriptures and spiritual writers. I have no doubt, for example, that at least 20 people in every congregation I preach to on a Sunday, could preach and teach better than I can. I look forward to a time when we will be able to share those gifts with the wider community.

25 July

The Salvation Army was founded by William Booth and his wife Catherine in 1865. Some of the good work the Salvation Army does in 111 countries throughout the world includes:

- One of the largest providers of Social Welfare in the world.
- It's the fifth largest charity in the UK.
- Worldwide it has 1.6 million members and 100,000 employees.
- It serves 3,000,000 meals every year at its various centres.
- They visit 79,000 prisoners in 131 prisons each year.
- They have 300 Youth Clubs providing care for young people.
- They run 70 Day Centres for elderly and disabled people.
- They also run residential centres for victims of alcohol and drug abuse and a centre for women trying to escape from domestic violence.

I could not have greater appreciation of the good work the Salvation Army does. Yet they are only one group of Christians who are the glue holding society together despite all our problems. The power of voluntary workers is truly amazing.

26 July

I'm beginning to suspect Gay Byrne's influence reaches to very high places indeed. How else could you explain the Vatican's sudden interest in good driving, road deaths and sinful ways to use the road? Here are their ten commandments and I hope you abide by them, especially if you are on the same road as I am.

10 Commandments for drivers:
1. You shall not kill.
2 The road shall be for you a means of communion between people and not of mortal harm.
3 Courtesy, uprightness and prudence will help you deal with unforeseen events.
4 Be charitable and help your neighbour in need, especially victims of accidents.
5 Cars shall not be for you an expression of power and domination, or an occasion of sin.
6 Charitably convince the young and not so young not to drive when they are not in a fit condition to do so.
7 Support the families of accident victims.
8. Bring guilty motorists and their victims together, at the appropriate time, so that they can undergo the liberating experience of forgiveness.
9. On the road, protect the more vulnerable party.
10. Feel responsible toward others.

27 July

Many in authority give the church a bad name. The People of God is a more gentle family to belong to. But we do need to belong somewhere. We can't do it on our own. Eucharist, Communion means union with. Our lives are short. It's a simple process. 'I came from the Father and I've come into the world and now I leave the world and go to the Father' (John 16:28). Like leaves on trees. Like saviours on crosses. Like me and you on our journey.

28 July

I got a bit of a shock when the Archbishop of Canterbury, Dr Rowan Williams, compared himself to Homer Simpson. The archbishop could be in for a rough ride. I remembered admitting that I was a fan of the Simpsons and watched them whenever I could. I wasn't prepared for the reaction.

Mad, shocking letters came tumbling in. They claimed Homer was a blasphemer. There was one from a student in Maynooth (I hope he never got as far as ordination although I suspect he did) saying that the Simpsons were anti-religion and those who watched it were guilty of mortal sin.

My point is that we should take these things with a great big pinch of salt. See the humour in them and as long as they are talking about religion and morality, they are helping us to do our work.

I think Homer had it right when he said: 'I am not a bad guy – I work hard and I love my kids. So why should I spend half my Sunday hearing about how I'm going to hell?' Still I can't imagine Homer dressed in a clerical collar just yet!

29 July

This is a silly season. So I want to share a letter a colleague sent me. It was probably doing the rounds on the web. One piece of advice – *please* read right to the end!

Dear friends,

It is important for men to remember that, as women grow older, it becomes harder for them to maintain the same quality of housekeeping as when they were younger. When you notice this, try not to yell at them. Some are oversensitive, and there's nothing worse than an oversensitive woman.

My name is Jim. Let me relate how I handled the situation with my wife, Peggy. When I retired a few years ago, it became necessary for Peggy to get a full-time job along with her part-time job, both for extra income. Shortly after she started working, I noticed she was beginning to show her age. I usually get home from the golf club about the same time she gets home from work.

Although she knows how hungry I am, she almost always says she has to rest for half an hour or so before she starts dinner. I don't yell at her. Instead, I tell her to take her time and just wake me when she gets dinner on the table.

When doing simple jobs, she seems to think she needs more rest periods. She had to take a break when she was only half finished mowing the lawn. I try not to make a scene. I'm a fair man. I tell her to get herself a nice, big, cold glass of freshly squeezed orange juice, and just sit for a while. And, as long as she is making one for herself, she may as well make one for me too.

I know that I probably look like a saint in the way I support Peggy. I'm not saying that showing this much consideration is easy. Many men will find it difficult. Some will find it impossible!

Nobody knows better than I do how frustrating women get as they get older. However, guys, even if you just use a little more tact and less criticism of your aging wife because of this article, I will consider that writing it was well worthwhile. After all, we are put on this earth to help each other.

Yours helpfully, Jim

Editor's Note:

Jim died suddenly on May 27 of a perforated intestine. The police report says he was found with a Callaway extra long 50-inch Big Bertha Driver II golf club jammed up his rear end, with barely 5 inches of grip showing and a sledge hammer laying nearby.

His wife Peggy was arrested and charged with murder. The all-woman jury took only 15 minutes to find her Not Guilty, accepting her defence that Jim accidentally sat on his golf club.

30 July

One of the saddest events that ever took place in the history of Irish showbusiness was when the Miami Showband were brutally murdered as they returned from a performance in Banbridge, Co Down. At the time I knew all the members of the band and was close friends with some of them.

One of the most original talents ever to grace an Irish stage was Fran O'Toole. He was a vivacious, wonderful performer, a gifted songwriter and a talented musician who was never allowed to achieve his full potential. He was killed on a lonely road just a few miles from where he entertained the dancers a few hours before. Killed with him was Brian Mc Coy, an absolute gentleman who was not only from the North of Ireland but was also a Protestant. Also killed was 23 year old Tony Geraghty from Stanaway Road in Dublin whose family are still involved on the music scene.

On a personal note, I also like to remember at this time the late Tom Dunphy, who was killed in a car accident on 29 July 1975. That week four young men who had helped to pioneer the whole showband era were buried. It's a week I'll never forget. Thirty years later I still feel a great sadness at the loss of so many friends.

31 July

I'm not really easily annoyed about things religious. But I have to say that when I'm doing wedding rehearsals I frequently become furious. I always say to the couple, 'At your wedding day you will receive under both species.' They look at me as if I have three heads. They have not a clue what I am talking about.

I then explain to them that they receive not only the sacred host but also the precious blood. Invariably the groom or one of the best-men has this ingenious idea which they think nobody else in the world had ever thought of before and they'll say, 'Ah Jaysus give us plenty of the wine.' Now that's the point when I would love to head butt them. We as a church have no problem giving communion to people with neither faith nor respect while we refuse to give communion to people from other churches who have a far better understanding and a far better respect for what the Eucharist is.

1 August

I got to know Mo Mowlan quite well when she was Secretary of State for Northern Ireland. She appeared on programmes I presented both on radio and television. She was a strong woman and took no prisoners in an interview. You had to be on your toes.

'How long will this interview be when it's broadcast?' I explained, 27 minutes exactly. 'Then we shall speak for 30 minutes so you cannot edit out all the best bits.' She had nothing to learn.

I met her in various places and on numerous occasions after that. She always knew me by my first name, always had a favour or two to ask and always enjoyed a bit of leg pulling.

I never met her after she left Northern Ireland but I was immensely sad when she died. She was precisely what was needed in Northern Ireland at the time. A God send.

2 August

It's not often someone writes personally about suffering from depression. So when I saw 'A Priest Battles With Depression', I realised that the writer was a very brave man indeed.

'When I was at my worst, just three considerations kept me from committing suicide. First there was the distress which this would cause my parents … Secondly, concern about the potential for scandal in a priest killing himself. Thirdly, the conviction to which I clung by my fingertips, that somewhere in the heart of darkness, was God. Even here, he had some purpose for me.'

He has written it down in the hope that he can encourage others who suffer from depression or any other psychological illness. 'You are not peculiar, there is nothing to be ashamed of in depression, and you are not alone. There is medical help available, which can make a huge difference to your life. Finally, and perhaps most importantly, the suffering of Christ is with you in your darkness, and he will bring good even out of the depths of your pain.'

I know that many people will see themselves in the words Fr Anthony has so bravely written.

3 August

According to a recent press release, the Vatican at last turned a profit after years of losing money.

In the breakdown of the Vatican's wealth, I noticed that the famous paintings by Michelangelo and Raphael are valued at $1 a piece in Vatican accounts. They could be worth billions, but who'd pay for them and how could you remove them?

Far more profitable to the Vatican are the 1000 flats it owns in Rome. It also has the world's largest library.

The Vatican is now cashing in on its own brand name. It has moved its department store out of the basement and into a former railway station behind St Peter's Basilica. It sells watches valued at $3000 and flat screen televisions. What precisely those have to do with religion is not easily seen. But the reorganisation has paid handsome dividends. What with Vatican stamps and memorabilia selling well last year, it made a profit of $2 million on a turnover of $210 million.

4 August

I was fascinated to learn the facts about this independent state called Vatican City. It is the only all-male state in the world. It has a population of 921, headed by Pope Benedict XVI. The Vatican is also the world's smallest state. With an all-male population, I wonder how they manage to have a 0.01% population growth.

It has no coastline, no natural resources; its main religion is Roman Catholicism. The most prominent ethnic groups are Italian and Swiss, with Italian and Latin being its main languages. Its government's style is ecclesiastical. Another word for dictatorship.

The population of the state quadruples every morning with the arrival of the 3000 lay people who work there.

5 August

Clifford Longley, writing in *The Tablet*, made an interesting point: 'A nun kneels to pray before the Blessed Sacrament, rosary in hand. What could be more Catholic? But you could almost say – what could be more Islamic? The rosary was originally the Muslim *Sibhah*, a string of prayer beads usually of amber, for counting prayers through the fingers. The Dominicans adapted it for Christian purposes in the 13th century.

The usual Catholic explanation of the Real Presence in the Blessed Sacrament, Transubstantiation, would never have been possible had not Thomas Aquinas and others absorbed Aristotle's metaphysics from the great Muslim philosophers ... Indeed Western medicine, philosophy, science, mathematics and architecture owe their place in the European Christian tradition entirely to such Arabic sources.

It is common nowadays to remark on the close relationship between Catholicism and Judaism, but it is arguable that the relationship with Islam is closer.'

6 August

One of the most tragic events in the world's history happened at 8.15am on 6 August 1945, when the atom bomb exploded over the people of Hiroshima. It destroyed everything within a radius of 5 kilometres. It caused a whirlwind that travelled at 1000 miles per hour and the heat reached 10,000° Celsius. Not unnaturally the devastation was horrific and at least 200,000 people were killed.

The survivors, even today, are bitter at the indifference of the West to their plight. Even worse, the young people in their own country are unaware of the tragedy and trauma they suffered.

Extraordinarily, there was hope in the midst of such evil. They recognised that life was beginning afresh when the leaves of the atomised trees began to grow again.

These are things that we should not forget. Great tragedies are carried out in the world today by evil people. We should remember though, and this is no justification for today's bombings, that the West has its own share of evil to repent.

7 August

It was fascinating to read how the papers treated World Youth Day in Cologne. Judging by reports it was a hugely successful event, with hundreds of thousands of young people from all over the world enjoying both the carnival like atmosphere and a memorable spiritual experience.

The *Daily Telegraph* had a more cynical view: 'The man who frequently condemns unbridled consumerism turned out on a recent break in The Alps in a quilted jacket, a £2,000 Cartier watch, Cartier glasses and a baseball cap.' In Cologne itself young pilgrims were able to buy Pope T-shirts with slogans (eg: Papa Ratzi), Pope teddy bears, a huge variety of candles, earrings, key rings, necklaces and crosses. There were even lollipops bearing the image of the Pope. John Paul II was cherry flavoured and Benedict tasted of herbs. Even Ikea offered pilgrims beds for the night but you had to assemble them yourself. A supermarket had beer glasses with photographs of the Pope engraved on them. The traders were expecting to make more than $20m on souvenirs alone.

And to think that Martin Luther left the church over the selling of indulgences!

8 August

I loved Benedict XVI's response when he was asked what part humour plays in the life of a Pope. He answered, 'I'm not a man who constantly thinks of jokes, but I think it's important to be able to see the funny side of life and its joyful dimension and not to take everything too seriously. I'd also say it's necessary for my ministry. A writer once said that angels can fly because they don't take themselves too seriously. Maybe we could fly a bit if we didn't think we were so important.'

9 August

Could you imagine *Imagine* corrupting a child's mind about religion? I thought not. Neither could I. Back when John Lennon wrote the song in the early 70s, people could be excused for not understanding what *Imagine* was saying. But 40 years later we should know that *Imagine* is not a song condemning religion, but rather condemning the abuses of religion which lead to war.

And yet a church school in England recently banned the children from singing *Imagine* at the end-of-term concert. The music teacher was backed by the headmaster who was backed by the local priest.

But almost everybody knows John Lennon was not saying 'don't believe' but was rather encouraging peace and love and was complaining about the number of people who were using religion to encourage war. 40 years ago I was often called into radio stations to defend lyrics such as *Imagine*. I gave it up after a short while. There's no point in defending lyrics. Either people get the message or they don't. Song lyrics are not meant to be theology. They are art or poetry. Imagine, here I am trying to defend *Imagine*. I should have more wit. Imagine that!

10 August

There is no good news from Benedict XVI with regard to women priests. 'We reflect a lot about this subject. As you know we believe that our faith and the constitution of the College of the Apostles binds us and doesn't allow us to confer priestly ordination on women. But we shouldn't think either that the only role one can have in the church is that of being a priest. There are lots of tasks and functions in the church.' He also pointed out that he'd like to bring women into decision-making roles but insists that canon law doesn't allow it. 'According to canon law the power to make legal binding decisions is limited to those in Sacred Orders.'

Has it not occurred to him that he could change canon law? It's interesting that he claims canon law and not divine law is the reason. But he does add, 'We will have to try and listen to God so as not to stand in their (women's) way, but on the contrary, to rejoice when the female element achieves the fully effective place in the church best suited to her, starting with the Mother of God and Mary Magdalene.'

11 August

I have heard it all now. Teachers in Britain have now been told to stop telling children they are clever, even when they are top of the class. The reason is that the rest of the class could give them a hard time because its 'un-cool' to be clever.

Any teacher who would follow that guide line is more stupid than the worst dunce in the class, in my opinion. But beware! If it happens in England some bright spark back from an educational junket will advise that schools everywhere should do it.

12 August

I heard a true story that happened here in Northern Ireland. A man was standing in the centre of a well known town when bus after bus of school children passed by from the Protestant and Catholic schools nearby and created a huge traffic block in the town. The old man was lying across the railing looking at these children, over a thousand in all, heading home from their schools.

He looked at the man beside him who, like himself, never had an opportunity to go to second level schools. He says, 'Tom, there'll be money for ignorance yet.'

13 August

Sometimes we can learn a lot about the preciousness of life from simple facts of nature. Only recently I learned that if there were no insects, most trees, plants, flowers and fruits would disappear from the planet. Furthermore, insects can thrive without us humans but we would perish without insects.

Did you know that a blink lasts exactly 0.3 seconds? A sneeze can travel about 100 miles per hour. All babies are colour blind at birth. The human heart will beat 2.5 billion times during a typical life span. Enamel is the hardest substance in the human body. A person has 2 million sweat glands. And girls have more taste buds than boys.

I don't know what all this has to do with anything. But maybe this little quotation from Vaclav Havel would give you hope for your journey: 'Hope is not the conviction that something will turn out well, but the certainty that something makes sense regardless of how it turns out.'

I like that.

14 August

I'll share an e-mail I got during the week. It's amazing what they write. A man wanted to get himself a new high performance car which would also be a status symbol. So he went to the local Redemptorist Monastery and he said, 'I want to buy a Lexus, would you say a Novena for me?' The priest asked him, 'What's a Lexus?'

'Oh it's a high performance car, a status symbol, and I want to get one and would you please say a Novena that I will get one?' The priest replied, 'Oh we wouldn't say a Novena for anything like that, but maybe if you go up to Ardoyne to the Passionists, they might.'

So off he went to the Passionists and presented his request. The Passionist said, 'We wouldn't say a Novena for a thing like that but if you go to Brian D'Arcy in The Graan he'll do anything.'

So off he went to The Graan and he met Fr Brian there and said, 'Fr Brian would you say a Novena for me? I want to get a Lexus.'

Fr Brian said, 'What's a Novena?'

15 August

In every relationship there are at least six people. Who you think you are; who the other thinks you are; who you really are; who she thinks she is; who you think she is; who she really is.

Whether we like it or not, people grow at a different pace. The danger is that unless there is a constant conversation going on, people will also grow to a different place.

Perhaps the most important word is the word love. That's worth thinking about. Did/does he/she love you? There are many relevant issues about duty, vows, entitlements and indeed compromise. But if mutual love is absent, what's the point of any relationship?

16 August

A survey carried out in Britain points out that working parents are now getting an average 40 minutes less sleep than they used to. They wake up earlier to travel to work and they cram more domestic activity in at the end of the day. Both father and mother are continually under pressure.

I thought the most interesting finding in the survey was that only 6% of working mothers want to be in fulltime employment. The ideal for the vast majority of mums in particular, was to be a mum who works part-time. Time to rest, time to recharge the batteries, time to just be together as a family is so precious that nothing should be more important.

By the way, not too many of them will read this because less than 20 minutes in every 24 hours is dedicated to reading and the vast majority of parents read less than 10 minutes a day!

17 August

The high cost of houses, with two mortgages, is destroying family life, and robbing parents and children of so much. Something has got to give. I love to see people have comfortable homes and having time to relax and have holidays. For too long we had nothing in this country. So I'm not one for condemning the Celtic Tiger or our lifestyle now.

But any sensible person would want to ask some questions. Why do we need such big houses for such small families?

I am always encouraged to see families spend time together at home and on holidays. Children want to be with their parents for a few short years. If their relationship isn't bonded during that time then everybody misses out.

18 August

St Vincent de Paul on God's mercy
'Always turn your eyes from the study of your own sin to the contemplation of God's mercy. Devote much more thought to the grandeur of his love for you than to your unworthiness toward him, to his strength than to your weakness. When you have done this, surrender yourself into God's arms in the hope that he will make you what he requires you to be and that he will bless all you do.' (quoted from *The Saints' Guide to Learning to Pray* by Louise Perrotta, Charts Press.)

St Vincent de Paul (1580-1660) was the founder of the Vincentians and co-founder of the Daughters of Charity. He is the patron saint of all charitable societies and works.

19 August

Ronald Rolheiser OMI on Mourning our losses

Perhaps the greatest spiritual and psychological challenge for us once we reach mid-life is to mourn our deaths and losses. Unless we mourn properly our hurts, our losses, life's unfairness, our shattered dreams, our radical inconsummation, and the life that we once had but that has now passed us by, we will live either in an unhealthy fantasy or an ever-intensifying bitterness. Spiritually we see an illustration of this in the story of the older brother of the prodigal son. His bitterness and unwillingness to take part in the celebration of his brother's return points to what he is still clinging to – life's unfairness, his own hurt, and his own unfulfilled fantasies. He is living in his father's house, but he is no longer receiving the spirit of that house. Consequently he is bitter, feels cheated, and lives joylessly ... Thus we have a choice: We can spend the rest of our lives angry, trying to protect ourselves against something that has already happened to us, death and unfairness, or we can grieve our losses, abuses, and deaths and, through that, eventually attain the joy and delights that are in fact possible for us. The choice is really a paschal one. We face many deaths within our lives, and the choice is ours as to whether those deaths will be terminal (snuffing out life and spirit) or whether they will be paschal (opening us to new life and new spirit). Grieving is the key to the latter. Good grieving, however, consists not just in letting the old go, but also in letting it bless us. (*The Holy Longing: The Search for a Christian Spirituality*, Doubleday)

Rolheiser is a Missionary Oblate of Mary Immaculate and writes a regular newspaper column on spirituality. He lives in Canada.

20 August

Recently a family who suffered a number of suicides came to see me in great distress. They had been advised by a neighbour to visit a 'medium' who could put them in contact with the three members of their family who had taken their own lives. These were vulnerable people in the throes of grief. They parted with a considerable amount of money to a person with no qualifications and, in my view, without scruples either. These people, in the midst of deep grief, were taken advantage of by a rogue. There is no other way of putting it.

21 August

A little boy had seen a lovely red bike in the local store and he demanded that his mother get it. The mother decided that he had to earn it. 'I'll make a bargain with you,' she said, 'If you can keep your room tidy, then we can discuss this again next Monday.' So the boy worked very hard at keeping his room clean. Several plastic bags were filled with rubbish and eventually a floor was discovered. Monday arrived and he thought he was sure to get his red bike.

The mother pointed out that that was only the start. He was doing very badly at school. 'If you study enough this week, then we'll talk about it next Monday.'

The young boy wasn't going to school for nothing. He knew this was a tactic that wasn't going to work so he thought he'd adopt more direct approach. He sat down to write a letter to God at his computer. So he began, 'Dear God, I'm the best boy in the world.' Even he knew that he wasn't the best boy in the world and since God knows all things God was likely to know that too. So he deleted and started again, 'Dear God, I'm as good a boy as you made me…' But he knew it mightn't work either.

He noticed a lovely statue of Our Lady in his mother's room. He went back to his computer and began to write, 'Dear God, if you ever want to see your mother again …'

22 August

Macrina Wiederkehr OSB on Real Presence
Everything can bless us, but we've got to be there for the blessing to occur. Being present with quality is a decision we are invited to make each day. It is another way to become like God. Due to the reality of our terribly distracted, cluttered and noisy existence, the decision for real presence is not easy. If we can make this decision and live it, it will be a kind of salvation for us. It can save us from many kinds of death: the death of apathy and mediocrity, the death of carelessness, the death of boredom, the death of selfishness, the death of meaninglessness. There is nothing so healing in all the world as real presence. Our real presence can feed the ache for God in others. (*A Tree Full of Angels: Seeking the Holy in the Ordinary,* HarperCollins)

23 August

Pierre Teilhard de Chardin on Redemptive suffering

What a vast ocean of human suffering spreads over the entire earth at every moment! Of what is this mass formed? Of blackness, gaps, and rejections. No, let me repeat, of potential energy. In suffering, the ascending force of the world is concealed in a very intense form. The whole question is how to liberate it and give it a consciousness of its significance and potentialities. The world would leap high toward God if all the sick together were to turn their pain into a common desire that the kingdom of God should come to rapid fruition through the conquest and organisation of the earth. All the sufferers of the earth joining their sufferings so that the world's pain might become a great and unique act of consciousness, elevation, and union. Would not this be one of the highest forms that the mysterious work of creation could take in our sight? Could it not be precisely for this that the creation was completed in Christian eyes by the Passion of Jesus? We are perhaps in danger of seeing on the cross only an individual suffering, a single act of expiation. The creative power of that death escapes us. Let us take a broader glance, and we shall see that the cross is the symbol and place of an action whose intensity is beyond expression.

24 August

I was reading recently that the Irish potato famine which occurred 1845-50 resulted in a 30% drop in the population of Ireland. The famine and the hunger broke the body and spirits of the population.

John Bloomfield was the owner of Castlecaldwell in Fermanagh. He noticed that his tenant farmers lived in small cottages but each had a vivid white finish. They told him that the clay deposit on his property had an unusually fine quality.

And so to generate revenue and provide employment on his estate, he built a pottery at the village of Belleek in 1857. The unusually fine clay yielded porcelain china that was almost translucent.

Belleek China was an immediate success and still is, one hundred and fifty years later. It's a thriving industry. It all arose because one man kept thinking positively in hard times.

25 August

Bob Woodrull is one of the best known journalists in America, both print and TV. Most recently he was the co-anchor of ABC's *World News Tonight*. In 2006, whilst he was covering the war in Iraq, he was travelling with a US army tank unit when a bomb went off. He and his camera men were hit. Bob suffered a serious brain injury which nearly killed him.

Bob and his wife Lee have written a book entitled, *In An Instant* about their experiences. Lee's story is vital because for five weeks after the operation which put Bob's head back together again, he was in a medically induced coma waiting for his brain to heal.

My favourite quote from *In An Instant* is where Bob and Lee reflect on the lasting effects the tragedy had on their four children:

'Our children will be more loving, more empathetic, more wonderful human beings than they are already for taking this unsuspected journey together, as a family. May you always remember that there are no perfect parents, just mothers and fathers doing the very best they can. There are no perfect spouses either, just those who love each other enough to stand by for better or worse. That kind of endurance is, perhaps, the greatest expression of love.'

26 August

The Lancet is the most reputable medical journal in the world. They reported on research that was commissioned by the British government. Cannabis is blamed for one in seven cases of schizophrenia.

The authors of the study put in plainly: 'We believe there is now enough evidence to inform people that using cannabis could increase their risk of developing a psychotic illness in later life.' It would be unfair to say that everyone who dabbles with drugs will develop a psychotic illness. That is plainly not true.

However, it would be utterly irresponsible to risk mental illness by abusing drugs like cannabis. You will never know if you are an alcoholic or not until you take your first drink. Equally so with drugs. It's only after you have dabbled with cannabis that you will discover whether you are one of those unlucky people whose mind will be destroyed by the stuff. That's why you shouldn't use it.

27 August

Abraham Lincoln was elected to Congress in 1846.
John F. Kennedy was elected to Congress in 1946.
Abraham Lincoln was elected President in 1860.
John F. Kennedy was elected President in 1960.
Lincoln's secretary was named Kennedy.
Kennedy's secretary was named Lincoln.
Andrew Johnson, who succeeded Lincoln, was born in 1808.
Lyndon Johnson, who succeeded Kennedy, was born in 1908.
John Wilkes Booth, who assassinated Lincoln, was born in 1839.
Lee Harvey Oswald, who assassinated Kennedy, was born in 1939.
Both assassins were known by their three names.
Both names are composed of fifteen letters.
Now hang on to your seat ...
Lincoln was shot at the theatre named 'Ford'.
Kennedy was shot in a car called 'Lincoln' made by 'Ford'.
Lincoln was shot in a theatre and his assassin ran and hid in a warehouse.
Kennedy was shot from a warehouse and his assassin ran and hid in a theatre.
Booth and Oswald were assassinated before their trials.
And here's the kicker ...
A week before Lincoln was shot, he was in Monroe, Maryland.
A week before Kennedy was shot, he was with Marilyn Monroe.

28 August

Some definitions which I hope will give you a laugh – and maybe a pause for thought as well:

Amen: The only part of a prayer that everyone knows.

Bulletin: Your receipt for attending church.

Choir: A group of people whose singing allows the rest of us to lip-sync.

Holy Water: A liquid whose chemical formula is H2OLY.

Hymn: A song of praise usually sung in a key three octaves higher than the congregation's range.

Recessional Hymn: The last song of the service, often sung quietly since most of the people have already left.

Incense: Holy Smoke!

Jonah: The original 'Jaws' story.

Justice: When kids have kids of their own.

Pew: A medieval torture device still found in Catholic churches.

Procession: The ceremonial formation at the beginning of the service consisting of servers, the readers, the celebrant, and late worshippers looking for seats.

Recessional: The ceremonial procession at the conclusion of the service led by the congregation trying to beat the crowd to the car park.

Ten Commandments: The most important Top Ten list not given by David Letterman.

Ushers: The only people in the church who don't know the seating capacity of a pew.

29 August

In an interview I once did with Peter Ustinov, he told me story which I think is true. His maternal grandfather was a Russian Jew. And he was slightly odd but a very wise old man who lived for a time with the Ustinov family. He brought with him as one of his possessions from his past, a rather ornate fly swat. And he proceeded to show the young Ustinov how to us it. He feebly attempted to swat flies but he was so slow and so ponderous about it that the flies had ample warning of his arrival and he never killed a single fly. Young Ustinov then took the fly swat and proceeded with his tennis ability etc to kill flies with great ease. The old man was furious. He took the swat back from him and then asked the young Ustinov why he had done this. He explained that flies were bad insects full of diseases and could kill people. They carried too many diseases. The old man looked at Ustinov and said, 'I'd much rather you'd suffer a little sickness than that you learn to kill too easily.' It's a salutary lesson.

30 August

The death of Lord Deedes brought memories flooding back to me. In the early 70s I was a newly ordained priest, in Dublin, who was given the task of rescuing a failing religious publication ominously entitled *The Cross Magazine*. I knew little about real journalism and nothing about editing, except perhaps that I should learn from the few gifted journalists I knew. I used every contact I had to get good writers to contribute.

At the time William Deedes was still in politics with a brief which included Northern Ireland. I wrote to him at Westminster and asked to meet him. With typical kindness he agreed and almost instantly he said he would be 'delighted' to write for my unimportant little magazine. Within two days 1000 words arrived in the post. Needless to say, they bore the hallmark of his sparse, vivid, clear, unostentatious style and were so controversial that they were subsequently widely quoted by other newspapers.

31 August

It's not often I quote Bill Gates. Here he gives advice to young people starting off in life. It's tough stuff but very helpful. These Ten Commandments are different:

1: Life is not fair – get used to it.

2: The world won't care about your self esteem. The world will expect you to accomplish something before you feel good about yourself.

3: You will *not* make £50,000 a year right out of school. You won't be a vice president with a car phone until you earn both.

4: If you think your teacher is tough, wait till you get a boss.

5: Flipping burgers is not beneath your dignity. Your grandparents had a different word for burger flipping – they called it opportunity.

6: If you mess up, it's your own fault. So don't whine about your mistakes, learn from them.

7: Before you were born, your parents weren't as boring as they are now. They got that way from paying your bills, cleaning your clothes and listening to you talk about how cool you thought you were.

8: Your school may have done away with winners and losers, but life *has not*. In some schools they have abolished failing grades and they'll give you as *many times* as you want to get the right answer. This doesn't bear the slightest resemblance to *anything* in real life.

9: Life is not divided into terms. You don't get summers off and very few employers are interested in helping you *find yourself*. Do that on your own time.

10: Be nice to nerds. Chances are you'll end up working for one.

1 September

I hope a man of the integrity and the ability of the great Sean Boylan is not lost to the GAA or to society.

I invited him once to speak in our church at The Graan in Enniskillen. He gave a fantastic, spiritually uplifting talk to a packed congregation. What impressed us all was that he never mentioned winning 4 All-Irelands, or Leinster titles or National Leagues or even Centenary Cups. No. He spoke of the suffering people who came to him and how they made him both humble and grateful.

That's the real Sean Boylan. I spoke to him on many occasions when my beloved Fermanagh had the temerity to beat his invincible Royals, and on a few occasions when Meath were victors too. He took both defeat and success with dignity and quickly moved on to ask about someone else who was sick. Football for him was everything during a game, but just a game in the context of life.

Thanks, Sean, for all the humour, kindness, honesty. And thanks too for the dignity you gave to football and to life.

2 September

Margaret Hebblethwaite describes what it's like to be poor in Chile. 'Being poor means that when you're in love with a girl in another town, you cannot ring her, you cannot visit her, you cannot even write letters to her because you cannot afford a stamp. What can hurt more than that?

'Being poor means that when your partner beats you up and leaves you with bruises all down your body, you cannot escape with your children to the safety of your mother's house because you cannot afford the £3 fare.

'Being poor means that when your girlfriend becomes pregnant and goes to live somewhere else in the country, you never know, even 20 years later, whether you had a child.

'Being poor as a child means that you go to school without breakfast and ask permission from your teacher to go home at breaktime in the hope that your father has found something for you to eat.'

(Margaret Hebblethwaite writing in *The Tablet*.)

3 September

Have you heard about the Stinking Bishop? I was fascinated to read that Charles Martell, a cheese maker and self confessed hippy, was less than impressed with the news that his homemade cheese is about to become world famous.

The cheese, called Stinking Bishop took a starring role in the Wallace and Gromit film. When another company's cheese appeared in another Wallace film, Wensleydal quadrupled its business. That's the last thing Charles Martell wants.

He's quoted as saying, 'I won't be able to cope. I don't know what is going to happen. We are a small firm, a micro business really, and we simply can't produce more cheese. I'm quite happy with what I have got at the moment. I don't need more money. I can only wear one suit at a time, or drive one car. And I certainly don't want fame.'

At the moment his company employs just two cheese makers and they produce about a hundred rounds a day.

Whatever about the Stinking Bishop, Martell certainly has his priorities right.

4 September

I was reading Nelson Mandela's autobiography, *Long Walk To Freedom*. During the cruel regime in Robben Island, an overseer came to talk to the prisoners. There was a man in charge called Captain Badenhorst, who made sure it was a brutal regime. And during the exchange of views Nelson Mandela, very bravely whilst still a prisoner, stood up and explained why the regime was so brutal. He didn't mention the Captain by name but it was obvious who he held responsible for it. To his surprise, the next day Captian Badenhorst called the prisoners together and told them he was leaving the prison that day. He went on to say that he wished everyone including Mr Mandela every blessing and every success for the future. Mandela admits that this shocked him more than anything. He was forced to reappraise Captian Badenhorst. And he said, 'All men, even brutal men have a core of decency.'

5 September

Ground Rules for Drinking:
1. Drink moderately.
2. Try to eat before and while drinking.
3. Sip slowly, never gulp.
4. Don't mix alcohol with other drugs.
5. Respect the right of those who choose to abstain.
6. Recognise that drunkenness is socially unacceptable.
7. Set limits to the number of drinks you decide to have and stick rigidly to it.
8. Discourage the 'rounds' system.
9. Never drink while driving or using machinery.
10. Respect alcohol – remember that in small amounts it gives pleasure to many, in excess it causes trouble.
11. Don't let alcohol become an essential part of living.
12. Avoid drinking in the daytime if possible.

6 September

I made a fleeting visit to New York where I was officiating at a marriage.

Americans feel guilty after hurricane Katrina. They can't understand how a nation, which helped the downtrodden all over the world, neglected so many poor blacks on their own doorstep. Apart from the huge number who died, probably close to one thousand, there are tens of thousands of refugees. They are being shunted from place to place and are joining the poor in other cities, looking for housing, food and jobs.

Sr Joan Chittister said: 'Have we come to the point where people count less in this country than inflating our international ego with space travel that eats up money and brings back rocks?' America is obviously worried about its roots and direction.

7 September

There is a lovely wee story about a husband who was worried that his wife was going deaf. This man went to the doctor because any suggestion that his wife might be getting old would not have been well received. He asked the doctor for help.

The doctor suggested a little experiment. Stand about fifteen feet away from your wife and ask her a question. If she answers it she is okay. If she doesn't then go a little bit closer and ask the same question. If she answers it she is probably okay but if she doesn't she might have some mild deafness. Finally go about three feet away from her and ask the same question. By that stage you will know how deaf she is.

At home his wife was dutifully cooking the evening meal. He stood at the dining room door:

'What have we got for tea this evening darling?'

There was no answer. So he went to the kitchen door:

'What have we got for tea this evening darling?'

No answer. Then he went right up to her, beside the cooker:

'What have we got for tea this evening darling?'

She gave him a look that would turn milk and snapped:

'I have told you three times already. It's roast chicken.'

8 & 9 September

This is Me

I accept myself completely.

I accept my strengths and my weaknesses,

My gifts and my shortcomings,

My good points and my faults.

I accept myself completely as a human being.

I accept that I am here to learn and grow, and

I accept that I am learning and growing.

I accept the personality I've developed, and

I accept my power to heal and change.

I accept myself without condition or reservation.

From this place of strength, I accept my life fully and I open to the lessons it offers me today.

I accept that within my mind are both fear and love, and

I accept my power to choose which I will experience as real.
I recognise that I experience only the results of my own choices.
I accept the times that I choose fear
as part of my learning and healing process, and
I accept that I have the potential and power
in any moment to choose love instead.
I accept mistakes as a part of growth,
so I am always willing to forgive myself and
give myself another chance.
I accept my own life as a blessing and a gift.
My heart is open to receive, and I am deeply grateful.
May I always share the gifts that I receive fully, freely, and with joy.
(Author Unknown)

10 September

The question I am asked most these days is: 'Why are so many young people taking their own lives?' I don't know the answer. The more I study the issue, the more I am convinced that no-one knows the answer. What I do know is that suicide is the Number One killer of Ireland's young men.

Teen-Line asked me to support their work by becoming one of their patrons.

Teen-Line specially targets young people, both male and female, between the ages of 13 and 19. They specifically want to help young people who are alone or who feel alone, worried, depressed, troubled, lost or confused. They are committed to improving the social and emotional help of all young people by offering a professional and caring service. Already they have developed a Teen-Line Ireland website and have a call service for Dublin which they hope to extend to regional centres.

11 & 12 September

I gathered a few youngsters and asked them how they would like their parents to behave. It doesn't mean parents have to behave this way. But glance through them and see what you think.

What follows is a list of some of the things they said, not in any particular order and certainly not in order of importance.

1   If you want to fight with us, please explain what the fight is about. Most fights are caused by not understanding what you mean. So please try to tell us clearly what we have done wrong.
2   Don't always stick your nose into what we are doing. If someone rings me, there is no need to ask every time 'Who is that?' We have a right to some privacy.
3   We like to be told we are good sometimes. Certainly we like rewards but we long for a word of appreciation. Remember you were a teenager once yourself and felt the same way as we do now.
4   When I do something wrong and there is a visitor in the house, particularly my friends, don't shout at me in front of them. If you have to give out wait until they are gone. It embarrasses them and me. It does you no good either.
5   There is no need to keep reminding us of the sacrifices you have made for us. We actually do talk about it and wonder if we will ever be able to do it for our children. We realise that your life is hard and we are part of that problem. But when you keep telling us what you had to give up, it seems to us to say, 'You have messed up our lives.' Sometimes it says, 'We really didn't want you.'
6   When I bring in one of my friends there is no need to ask, 'What does your father do?' Does it really matter? When you behave well to our friends, we are proud to have you as parents. When you mess up, we have to explain you away.
7   Our music may be junk to you but we like it. As a matter of fact we are not too keen on your stuff either but we are prepared to live and let live. Anyway if you listen enough you might actually find a clue on how we think. Some of them even have advice for you. Often when I play a record it is to get you to listen to how I think, because you wouldn't listen to me directly.

8 A sure way to turn us off is to start with, 'When I was your age.' The fact is we can't imagine you ever being our age. And if you think about it you never were our age, because the world has changed so much in the meantime.

9 We appreciate that sometimes you are in a foul mood. As teenagers we know only too well how unpredictable moods can be. It would help if both of us were able to talk about it and allow each other space and peace.

10 I know this is a ridiculous suggestion, but there could be times when you are wrong. It helps when you admit it, then we can be friends. And when I am wrong I can learn from you that it is no big deal.

11 Have repeated conversations about sex with us. One talk isn't enough because we are embarrassed to take much in. It might be helpful to have a number of talks so we can get through the embarrassment and maybe have a frank exchange. You might not like what you are going to hear though. The alternative is that we listen to you, ignore you and do what we want anyway. Maybe you are happy with that. But does it have to be that way?

12 This may be the hardest one of all. And as you know this is not a gripe list, it is trying to be helpful. So could you please read this next sentence? Even though we love you and want to do our best for you, even though we want to be friends, the fact is we are separate human beings, with our own lives to lead. The greatest tribute we as children can pay to you as parents, is that you raise us well enough to stand on our own two feet.

13 September

Fr Timothy Radcliffe says: 'Seeking the good is not primarily about rules and commandments. It is not about what one is obliged or forbidden to do. Thinking that morality is all about command- ments is a relatively new way of thinking, since the Reformation.' And he quotes no less an authority than St Thomas Aquinas, who saw morality as primarily about making a journey towards God and happiness. What was central was not the commandments but the virtues.

14 September

President Mary Mc Aleese has the rare skill of being able to speak profound thoughts in simple phrases. Here's an example:

'It is a necessary condition of growing up that we learn from our mistakes.'

'To be human is to change and to be perfect is to have changed often,' said Cardinal Newman. But change of itself is not enough for we are just as capable of changing for the worse as for the better and the process of growing up insists that we should get better, wiser, less capricious, more resilient. For change to mean 'growing up' we need to see how changes, including setbacks, and our responses to setbacks, lead us forward along a path.

15 September

The founder of L'Arche, Jean Vanier, says that Europe needs compassion and forgiveness.

'Compassion is lived when each of us bends down and welcomes the person who is lonely, lost and in need …

'Compassion is healing for the one who receives compassion but also for the one who gives compassion. Both persons are transformed.

'Compassion implies wisdom. Do not dive into the sea to save a drowning person unless you have a rope to hang onto. That rope is wisdom. We must not sink into the suffering of others but help the suffering person to find life's meaning.

'Compassion implies that we see the person behind the label of difference, pain, sickness or weakness and move from a sense of superiority and power to a relationship of friendship and mutual vulnerability.

'As we seek to be compassionate for the one who is lost, lonely and in pain, we learn to be compassionate in our own brokenness.'

16 September

When I was in New York for the Country Music Awards, I went to see the World Trade Centre being restored. Quite close by there is an old Anglican Church which has become world famous. It's St Paul's Church and it has stood there for 250 years.

While I was in St Paul's I read this reflection on a wall:

'I was hungry ... not for food because the freezer was full; I was hungry for a word of encouragement and all you did was point out my mistakes.

'I was a stranger ... not because I was in a foreign land but because you made me feel strange and different. It is a terrible crime to be different.

'I was thirsty ... not for drink because there was water in the tap but because my mouth was dry with fear. I wanted someone to listen to me and the television was more interesting than I was.

'I was naked ... not because I had no clothes but because your criticism stripped me of my self-esteem. I was naked without my good name.'

As I have often said before, perhaps the last line should read, 'I was saved by the hundreds of good people who loved me anyway.' And that's the truth too.

17 September

I know of no death which causes more sadness, more anger, more confusion than suicide. It leaves feelings of guilt and helplessness. We wonder how we could have helped somebody who took their own life and yet, no matter how closely we examine a suicide, we usually come to the conclusion that there was nothing we could have done because we didn't know what was going on inside their heads.

There is no infallible way to read the signs of a person about to take their own life. But there are warning signs which should not go unheeded. Those closest to the person usually see some signs, but I have sat with countless parents whose children took their own life without giving a single sign that they were in despair.

My best advice is simply to be a good listener. People at risk can send out warning signs. Many don't, so don't feel guilty if you don't pick them up.

18 September

It can help to allow people to talk about suicide. At least it gives you a chance to point out the foolishness of such an act and how devastating it is for those who are left behind. Don't under estimate the healing power of listening without judging. 'When everything comes at once it must get on top of you,' or, 'You must feel utterly helpless,' are good phrases. It allows the person to tell you about their feelings.

It is important that all of us know our limits. We cannot make choices for others. We cannot live their lives for them or keep them alive if they are determined to die. The best we can do is keep them alive long enough to get help. And there are times when we have to be a little cruel to be kind. If you feel someone close to you is considering suicide as a real option tell a professional who will be able to help them.

Take them to somebody who can help even if it means the emergency room of your local hospital. You may need to call the police because they have the power to bring a suicidal person to a place where their mental health can be assessed. Your friend will probably never forgive you for doing it, but at least they have a better chance of receiving help that will keep them alive.

19 September

You Are Beautiful.
Treat yourself the way you are, and you will remain so.
Treat yourself the way you can become, and you will become so.
Think freely. Smile often.
Tell those you love that you do.
Hope, grow, give, give in.
Pick some daisies. Keep a promise.
Laugh heartily. Enjoy. Trust life.
Reach out. Let someone in.
Make some mistakes. Learn from them.
Explore the unknown. Believe in yourself.
Celebrate your life! You are beautiful.

20 September

Of all the people I've met Mother Teresa of Calcutta was the most challenging. I interviewed her at least five times and regarded her as a living saint. Strangely though, she always left me feeling uncomfortable, that I was wasting my life, compared to the heroic work she was doing.

The last time I met her I began to change my mind. She told me, in quite a sharp way, that God didn't expect me to do her work, but rather that God wanted me to do my own work more wholeheartedly. Then she shocked me when she added: 'There are times when I think God is absent from my life and my work. I wonder if I'm doing any good at all.' She was deadly serious too and it has been a great comfort to me since, that even a saint like Mother Teresa was plagued with doubts about her own life and work.

21 September

President Mary Mc Aleese says that one of the challenges facing Europe today is the search of happiness. There are many indicators of unhappiness in Europe. Like voter apathy, cynicism, declining birth rate, increasing suicide rate particularly among the young and elderly, abuse of drugs lawful and unlawful; racism, road rage, and a Europe, 'where many of the elderly live lives of quiet loneliness'.

Yet we must also admit that there are many reasons to be grateful for the Europe we live in. 'Our world is full of second chances, of new, insistent voices telling us their story, setting out their ambitions, driving us on to deal with each other more humanly, more lovingly, more carefully … And if the generations had a choice of which generation they would be born into, many of those who have gone before us would join the queue for our generation …'

22 September

There is a new book on the private correspondence between Mother Teresa of Calcutta and her spiritual guides. It shows that the nun we all thought had a direct line to God, in her own life felt no trace of God's presence whatsoever. Teresa always seemed joyful and at peace when I met her, but deep down she felt so low and so useless that she compared the experience to hell. At one point she writes that she doubts the very existence of heaven and even of God.

For many this will come as a complete shock. If Mother Teresa doubted God, what chance is there for us? But there is another way of looking at it. I believe that the opposite of faith is not doubt but certainty. If I'm certain about everything there is no need for faith. On the other hand, it takes great faith to keep on struggling even though I don't know why I'm doing it.

Faith is not a feeling but a conviction that God is always there. Jesus on the cross thought God was absent too.

23 September

I find that unconditional love is admirable in others but almost impossible to practise myself. And yet the longer I think about it the more I realise that if I am to be anything like what God wants me to be, I have to love unconditionally because that's how God loves me. I don't see God as a control freak or a benign puppeteer either. I can't believe God is someone who manipulates me by jerkily pulling the strings of my life. God leaves us free to be ourselves because we're good people the way God made us. We might fail but he still loves us. We can deny him as Peter did and he'll always give us a fresh start.

No matter how hard it is for me, I have to try to love others in the same forgiving way as God loves me. I am not good at it but I have to try it. A reader dropped me a card which sums up what I'm trying to say:

'Live your life in such a way that those who know you, but don't know God, will come to know God, because they have known you.'

Simply put, but hellishly hard to live by.

24 September

Marcel Marceau was on my mind earlier in the month and I couldn't decide whether he was alive or dead. The first time I saw him in Dublin, I was asked to bring along the then Superior General of The Passionists, Fr Theodore Foley, a big warm, gentle, American priest. In the early 70s, to be Superior General was the next best thing to being Pope. And as the junior priest in Mount Argus I was asked to entertain him during one of his visits. Not knowing how to entertain minor Popes, I booked tickets for the Olympia Theatre and spent the night near the front row admiring the genius of Marcel Marceau.

The Superior General loved the show. He told me afterwards that it was one of the most brilliant shows he'd ever seen.

Earlier this month the same Fr Theodore Foley had his cause for canonisation introduced in Rome. I hope some day he will be a saint, because I rather like the idea of a saint who could see the genius of a clown for whom words were 'a kind of betrayal,' to paraphrase Heaney.

25 September

Ten Spiritual Tonics
1. Stop worrying. Worry kills life.
2. Begin each day with a prayer. It will arm your soul.
3. Control appetite. Over indulgence clogs mind and body.
4. Accept your limitations. All of us can't be great.
5. Don't envy. It wastes time and energy.
6. Have faith in people. Cynicism sours the disposition.
7. Find a hobby. It will relax your nerves.
8. Read a book to stimulate imagination and broaden your views.
9. Spend some time alone, for the peace of solitude and silence.
10. Try to want what you have instead of spending your strength trying to get what you want.
(Abraham Feinberg)

26 September

Imperfection will always be part of the human condition and since the church is peopled by humans, all churches have as many imperfections as gifts.

I should not expect any institution, least of all the church, to run smoothly. I should remember the lesson of the gospel. In a field of wheat, cockle and weeds grow side by side. It is beyond human power to separate them. We have to let them grow together and in time they will separate themselves. That's the gospel truth.

In the church the more enthusiasm we have, the more likely we are to run up against small minds, rigid minds, narrow minds, and stony hearts.

Even if we are lovers of order we are just as likely to be frustrated by the spirit blowing where the spirit will.

Our churches and our lives will always be untidy, riddled with contradictions. There will always be a sinful side and a virtuous side, a dark side and a bright side, a despairing side and one full of hope.

We shouldn't be surprised if the people of God are imperfect simply because people are imperfect.

27 September

'Man often becomes what he believes himself to be. If I keep on saying to myself that I cannot do a certain thing, it is possible that I may end by becoming really incapable of doing it. On the contrary, if I shall have the belief that I can do it, I shall surely acquire the capacity to do it, even if I may not have it at the beginning.'

— *Mahatma Gandhi*

28 September

'At Home With The Clearys' has left me deeply disturbed and even more confused, if that were possible. The fact that over half a million people tuned in late on a Monday night to watch the programme shows that, in death, as in life, Fr Michael Cleary is as controversial as ever. There is/was no better man to steal the limelight.

But a good man who was clear about so many things, he certainly left a mess behind him in his personal life.

The most sympathy has to go to his son Ross. He has been caught in the web that wasn't of his own making. It almost destroyed him. Phyllis, his mother, died less than eight years after Michael and left Ross orphaned at a relatively young age. For any young man that would be a difficult task. But when your father was the most famous priest in Ireland and your life was surrounded by secrecy and controversy, it's amazing that he survived at all.

For the Cleary family it has been a tragic and horrendous 14 years and, just when they thought that the controversy had faded into history, then 'At Home With The Clearys' resurrects all the passion and all the judgemental attitudes again.

If the programme showed anything it was that Michael Cleary's work was blessed because he knew the realities of family life. It showed that he could have been a wonderful father, husband and priest.

Sadly there are still far too many wonderful priests having to walk away from their vocation to accept God's even more wonderful gift of love.

Even five years ago, I believed that things would change and we would have decent married men accepted as priests, (and hopefully married women in the future). But now all I see is a dysfunctional and out of touch priesthood doing their best to appear real in a world that neither understands nor appreciates what our role, if any, is. And that's what makes me sad.

29 September

Ann Dempsey writes, in the teenage magazine *Face-Up*, on how to tackle love, sex and relationships. She gives these six good reasons to take your time with the S-word.

1. It's a myth that everyone's at it.

   The media – and even your mates – can give the impression that everybody's doing it. They're not. Many people make false boasts in research surveys, so even statistics are an exaggeration of the truth. Don't feel pressured into having sex just because you think it's the thing to do.

2. You have the right to say 'no'.

   Some girls believe they have to sleep with a boyfriend to prove they care about him. Not so. In fact, a boy who puts that kind of pressure on you isn't worth being with.

3. You're in control of your actions, not your mates.

   Some boys come under pressure from their friends to sleep with their girlfriend so that they can boast about it afterwards. Don't give in to this kind of pressure. It disrespects both you and the girl you care about.

4. It's okay to be curious without going any further.

   It's natural to be curious about sex. Talking about sex and making sexual jokes are part of your world, while films, books and TV can be sexually explicit. Curiosity is fine, but in the midst of all the messages, hold on to your own beliefs about what you want to do about sex.

5. The consequences can be devastating.

   Sexual experimentation can lead to sexually transmitted infections and having sex can lead to an unplanned pregnancy. Would you really want to be a parent at 16?

6. Sex isn't a measure of your worth.

   With today's obsession with sex, it's easy to assume that if you're not being sexual, you're behind the times. But a too-young sexual relationship can lead to a lot of unhappiness and tragedy. Take your time.

30 September

Francis of Assisi saw God's love in creation. He talked about brother sun and sister moon. What he thought centuries ago has become fashionable today. He said everyone has a dignity because everyone is a child of God.

Holiness does not come from doing good. Rather we do good because we are holy.

Holiness is not the avoidance of evil. Rather we avoid evil because we are holy.

Holiness is not the result of constant prayer. We pray because we are holy.

Holiness is not a gift we obtain after a lifetime of service. Rather we give service because we are holy.

Jesus said it all in Matthew's gospel when he said: 'I was hungry and you gave me food. I was thirsty and you gave me drink. I was a stranger and you welcomed me. I was naked and you gave me clothing. I was sick and you took care of me. I was in prison and you visited me ... As long as you did it to one of my brethren, then you did it to me.'

1 October

Bono was asked if he believed life is all there is, or did he believe in an after life? 'I will be very disappointed if this is all there is. I am having such a great life. I am never surprised at the ugliness in the world, nor by the beauty of it. I do think they are the eternal things. I love the idea of hell as a flame that will burn away all the crap and only the precious stones will remain. I think that's probably where things get evened out and I think that's probably what that idea of the first will be last means ... I feel I have a lot of faith. Musicians tend to have a lot of faith. When you hear one note in your head you have to have faith that there is another one around the corner.' (*Ten Eternal Questions* compiled by Zoe Sallis, Duncan Baird Publishers London)

2 October

Over 60 years ago Cicely Saunders was an inexperienced nurse in a London hospital. In her ward there was a young Polish waiter with no family or friends, dying of cancer. The medics concluded there was 'nothing more that could be done for him'. She couldn't accept that hospitals should lose interest in a person if they couldn't be cured. There should be more to life than that. She did her best to ease his pain before he died.

She must have been effective because in his will he left her £500 with the mysterious message 'to provide a window for your home'.

Today there are hospices everywhere and I spend many hours visiting them as part of my work. It all began when a young nurse had compassion for a lonely Polish patient dying alone. That's why at the entrance to St Christopher's hospice there is a window dedicated to the waiter whose £500 Will inspired a nurse's vision. As I frequently say: Good people are those who do ordinary things extraordinarily well.

3 October

I still feel embarrassed appearing in *VIP* magazine. When they first approached me I said no. But having talked it over with a good number of close friends, they convinced me to do it, on the basis that I have always tried to be part of the marketplace. It may be a foolish principle, but it's the only one I can have an easy conscience with as a priest today.

The reaction since it has been predictable. Some of my acquaintances have found it a little embarrassing, almost yuppie. But the vast majority have been supportive. Those who live in the real world understand what it's about. They see it as another attempt to be honest about my personal life and about the issues that matter in people's lives.

Everything is a learning experience and this one was more challenging than most. Maybe that's why I was relieved that it turned out as well as it did, though I still have a problem about what makes anyone a VIP.

4 October

The following words were found inscribed on the tomb of an Anglican Bishop who was buried in Westminster Abbey.

'When I was young and free and my imagination had no limits, I dreamed of changing the world.

As I grow older and wiser I discovered the world would not change. So I shortened my sights somewhat and decided to change only my country. But it too seemed immovable.

As I grew into my twilight years in one last desperate attempt, I settled for changing my family, those closest to me, but alas they would have none of it.

And now as I lie on my deathbed, I suddenly realise: if I had only changed myself first, then by example I would have changed my family.

And from their inspiration and encouragement I would have been able to better my country and, who knows, I may even have bettered the world.'

5 October

I was not looking forward to the *Ferns Report*. Even now it is barely thinkable that the people who claim to be the guardians of faith and morals allowed the evil destruction of beautiful innocent children over a period of at least 30 years, not only in Ferns but in dioceses and orders throughout the world.

The *Ferns Report* details a prolonged and shocking crisis. It highlights the flaws of the system which is supposed to protect children and the corruption that is at every level of the church's hierarchical structures. When we take it in conjunction with the even more devastating reports from Boston and Philadelphia, we see that this is no longer confined to a small section of the church's ministry.

All leaders in the church, myself included, must take responsibility for what we have done and failed to do. We have poisoned the life we were supposed to witness to. It's an old clerical trick to put your head down, say nothing, and hope it will go away. It is precisely that attitude which has allowed the rape and abuse of innocent children.

6 October

A Life Perspective
If God was to grant you 70 years of your life,
you would spend:

    24 years sleeping
    14 years working
    8 years in amusement
    6 years at the dinner table
    5 years in travelling
    4 years in conversation
    3 years in education
    3 years reading
    3 years watching television

If you went to church every Sunday and prayed 5 minutes every morning and night, you would be giving God 5 months of your life.

Can't we give 5 months out of 70 years?

7 October

'Every gun that is made, every warship launched, every rocket fired, signifies a theft from those who hunger and are not fed, those who are cold and are not clothed.

'The world in arms is not spending money alone. It's spending the sweat of its labourers, the genius of scientists, the hopes of its children ...'

(President Dwight D Eisenhower, 1953)

8 October

Change is difficult to effect. I remember hearing a story about a church which had a row of seats on which nobody ever sat. It had become a tradition that there was something special about this row. If visitors sat there by accident ushers would ask them to leave the seats because this was a sacred space.

Legends grew as to why this was such a sacred place. One tradition held it was reserved for the presence of Jesus. Others said it was something more sinister – that people had sat there and some evil had befallen them because they did. There were as many legends as there were people.

Recently the village and the congregation grew as a result of a new housing estate. So the minister decided to get to the bottom of the mystery. After days going through the parish records he found an entry written by one of his predecessors over 80 years earlier. It said that, 'The parish doesn't have enough money to fix the leak in the roof so we covered the fifth pew with a sheet to protect it. A bucket was placed on the pew to catch the water.' Years after the roof was repaired, people still avoided the fifth pew and found a 'holy' reason to justify a tradition.

Custom and tradition are mixed blessings. They can be wise guides to the future, or they can handcuff us to the past. No wonder Jesus condemned those 'who worship only with their lips while their hearts are far from me'.

9 October

October is the month when we celebrate the harvest. We thank God for the produce of the earth. We look around at the luscious fruits. The wholesome vegetables, the beautiful flowers. The sights and smells turn our heads and we can say with the Prophet Joel, 'Be glad and rejoice for the Lord has done great things.' We thank God for the earth we live in. We thank God for the air we breathe, that fills our lungs with life and strength. We thank God for the land that produces fruits and vegetables. We thank God for the abundance of water. We thank God for the animals that provide us with milk and meat, clothing and sometimes companionship.

We shouldn't forget either all the workers throughout the world who have planted, cared for, and harvested the crops and reared the animals. We offer back with thanksgiving that which God has given us and we praise God for his goodness.

10 October

There are times in life when everything is hopeless and yet when we've lived through them there is a sense that having fought the good fight, there's nothing left to do but to experience God's help. In our brokenness, we allow God to help us more than in times of strength. I know many people who have prayed whole-heartedly for a cure but who eventually succumb to death. There was a satisfaction that having prayed as diligently as we did, there was nothing else we could do. We did our best. We didn't get the result we wanted, but because we did all we could, there must be a reason for it.

11 October

Talking about football and footballers, the great Bill Shankey said this in his autobiography:

'I have left until last the major factor in any player's climb up the football ladder.

That is the simple question of courage. Some people seem to think I mean physical ability. Nothing could be further from the truth. Courage is a big word, it covers a multitude of accomplishments, just as much mental as physical, indeed perhaps more so.

'Courage is more than being able to stand up to a buffeting on the field of play. Courage is also the ability to get up when things are getting you down, to get up and fight back. Never to know defeat, let alone accept it; to have principles, be they of fitness or morality, and stick by them; to do what you feel what you must do, not because it is the popular thing to do but because it is the right thing to do.

'Courage is skill, plus dedication, plus fitness, plus honesty, plus fearlessness. It is a big word but it is one which should hang above your bed if you really want to be a professional footballer, and to be one that is a credit to the game and yourself.'

I have rarely read a more complete Mission Statement for a successful life than that.

12 October

Religion is not dead yet, despite everything we've done to destroy it. Faith continues to grow in the hearts of believers. I know because I have been privileged to spend a few days in Lourdes.

There have been articles written giving the impression that Lourdes is the new Ibiza. I'm sure you could find booze-ups if you looked hard enough to find them.

As I looked around me I saw no sign of drunken parties or of anything remotely resembling Ibiza. What I did see were thousands of very sick and dying people in a constant stream of wheelchairs, most of which had two young voluntary helpers giving up a week of their holidays to look after the sick and needy. I saw service at its best. I saw faith in action. I saw charity and love. And it gave me hope.

13 October

Did you hear about the grand old lady who was in Court for the first time at the age of 83 recently? The Prosecuting Counsel tried his best to make her feel at home in the strange surroundings of the courtroom. 'Mrs Smith, you know me don't you?' he began.

'Of course I know you, you're Donald Jones. I have known you since you were in nappies. You think you're the most important barrister in the country, but behind it all you are the same young delinquent teenager who broke into our orchard and stole our best apples every September. Your poor mother never had a moment's peace with you.'

'Now, now Mrs Smith,' Mr Jones said, trying to talk above the laughter echoing around the room, 'Try to keep you answers brief and to the point. Do you know that man over there?' He pointed to the Defence barrister.

'Yes I do,' Mrs Jones replied disdainfully. 'That's William Murphy whom everybody knows to be a cheat, a gambler and he drinks too much as well.'

Mr Murphy buried his face in his hands. The judge lifted his gavel and pounded the bench to restore order. He called the prosecuting barrister to the bench and in an audible whisper said, 'Mark my words, if you ask her whether she knows me,' the judge snarled, 'I'll have you thrown in jail for contempt immediately.'

14 October

In moments of doubt I have learned to cope by trying to remember a time in my life when God was tangibly present. There's not a person in the world who hasn't had an experience of somebody up there looking over them. Hold onto that. Make it a central part of your life. Go back to that place often. It's like the time when Jesus took his friends up to the top of a mountain and showed them heaven. His great suffering came immediately after, but the memory of that glimpse of heaven kept them going. The same can happen each of us.

15 October

A tribute to the bathrobe

There is no more comfortable and comforting garment in our closets than the bathrobe. When it comes to bathrobes, the bigger, the thicker, the warmer – the better.

The bathrobe keeps us gentle. It is possible to sulk in the bathrobe – but not to rage. Trying to be serious or authoritative in the bathrobe would be a joke, commanding neither respect nor fear…. Bad tempered, suspicious people never wear bathrobes and if they do, they shouldn't.

You are most yourself in your bathrobe. You are at your most vulnerable; you are at the mercy of others in a bathrobe. Putting on your bathrobe means taking off your pomposity and self importance.

You are at your most giving and forgiving in your bathrobe.

Bathrobes are made for cuddling, not arguing. Bathrobes embrace us in a spirit of blissful peace and unconditional love. Presidents and Prime Ministers, generals and leaders, should wear bathrobes at all times.

(Barbara Holland quoted in *Connections*, May 2007)

16 October

Glenveagh is a wonderful place to visit. A fantastic castle, beautiful walks, stunning views and an amazing history. Manicured and wonderful gardens, 22 acres in all, golden eagles, and red deer.

When our wee pilgrimage group got there, we went to the lake shore. We paddled our way to the rocks sitting at the side of the lake. The only sound that could be heard was the lapping of water. There are no birds in Glenveagh because the eagles drive them out.

It was exactly as one would have imagined the gospel scene of Jesus on the shore calling the disciples, having a meal with them and offering Eucharist with them. Few words were needed. We became aware of God's presence in nature. And once one became aware of it, there was no need for anything else.

It has been said that God's first scripture was his creation. There is no doubt about it, God speaks to us still through his creation.

17 October

I remember reading years ago that the phrase, 'Whatever you bind on earth will be considered bound in heaven, and whatever you loose on earth shall be considered loosed in heaven,' (Matthew 16-19) referred to more than forgiving sins in the Sacrament of Reconciliation. It does mean that. But a scripture scholar made what I think is a valid point when he argued: 'The same power is given to the whole Christian community.'

What it means in practice is that if a father and a mother, who remain part of the Christian community, forgive their children, then the children will also be forgiven before God. It means that if we love someone and hold them in our life, there is a sense in which that person cannot be cut off from the love of Christ. If we continue to love someone, they are bound up in our love.

What it could mean for many parents today is that their love and prayers will keep even wayward children within God's love and forgiveness. As long as the Christian community and their parents love them and forgive them, they will remain part of God's kingdom because of our love.

To put it bluntly, if we as human beings can see the goodness in a person, irrespective of their habits, then God who sees everything will find it easier than us to forgive them and bring them to heaven.

18 October

When The Dalai Lama visited Corrymeela in 2005 he told Alf Mc Creary a story which explains the need for reconciliation. He said: 'A friend of mine was released by the Chinese authorities in Tibet after a long period of imprisonment and torture. He said to me, "There is only one thing I now fear. I am afraid that I will not be able to forgive my captors. If I go on carrying a resentment against them that will not do any harm to the Chinese authorities but in the long-term that resentment will destroy me".'

(*In War And Peace, The Story of Corrymeela* by Alf McCreary, Brehon Press.)

19 October

'Where is God? God is where we are weak, vulnerable, small and dependent. God is where the poor are, the hungry, the handicapped, the mentally ill, the elderly, the powerless.

'How can we come to know God when our focus is elsewhere on success, influence and power? I increasingly believe that our faithfulness will depend on our willingness to go where there is brokeness, loneliness and human need.

'If the church has a future, it has a future with the poor in whatever form. Each one of us is very seriously searching to live and grow in this belief, and by friendship we can support each other. I realise that the only way for us to stay well in the midst of many 'worlds' is to stay close to the small, vulnerable child that lives in our hearts and in every other human being ...'
(from *Sabbatical Journey* by Henri Nouwen.)

20 October

I was walking earlier this morning in this beautiful Fermanagh countryside. The leaves crunched under my feet, the air was crisp and the sky pale blue. I puffed and panted as I pushed my aging body up the hillside. I turned around to take in the magnificent autumn view when I reached the top. That was when I thanked God for 'this little glimpse of eternity' in my own backyard.

21 October

Growing older gives us time for both more and less.
— More time for good memories, less times for nostalgia, pretending the past was any better than the present.
— More time to revel in living, with less time worrying about how to make a living.
— More time for satisfaction with what we have achieved, and less time worrying about what we have not done.
— More time to spend with a great book as we waste less time keeping up with ads.
— More time walking in fields with less time running in place.
— More time to get to know ourselves, as we spend less time wondering what everyone else thinks about us.
Finally, we may mourn more as we grow older, but be sure there are times to dance for joy too.
(The Christophers)

22 October

I have put forward the idea that the church ordain, for a start, good married men in the local community so that the Mass remains a central part of what it is to be a Catholic.

The Dominicans in Holland take that proposal a few steps further. It seems to me that the Holy Spirit throughout the church is asking us to have as serious look at priesthood itself. It's not just all about filling gaps.

A small step would be obvious. Allow priests to marry and ordain married men as priests. They don't have to be fulltime priests either. The whole structure of the church is changing. It's moving away from the evil of clerical power groups to a more broadly based People of God. The sooner it happens the better.

23 October

A wise Guru was so impressed by the spiritual progress of his pupil that he decided he needed no further guidance. He left him on his own in a little hut by the banks of a river and moved on.

Each morning, after washing himself, the young pupil would hang out his loin cloth to dry. It was his only possession. One day he was dismayed to find it torn to shreds by rats. And so he had to beg for another loin cloth from the villagers.

When the rats nibbled holes in this one too, he got himself a kitten. He had no more trouble with the rats but now, in addition to begging for his own food, he had to beg milk for the cat as well.

He thought it was too much of a burden on the villagers, so he decided to keep a cow.

When he got the cow he had to beg for fodder. Eventually, he got embarrassed and decided it was easier to till the land around his hut. But that proved troublesome and it left him very little time for his meditation. So he employed workers to till the land for him.

Over-seeing the workers became such a chore that he married a wife to share the task with him.

Before long he was one of the wealthiest men in the village.

24 October

At the beginning of the play, *Shadowlands*, C. S. Lewis, in a long talk directly to the audience, sets the scene: 'God creates us free, free to be selfish, but he adds a mechanism that will penetrate our selfishness and wakes us up to the presence of others in the world and that mechanism is called "suffering". To put it another way, pain is God's megaphone to rouse a deaf world …

'Self-sufficiency is the enemy of salvation. If you are self-sufficient, you have no need of God. If you have no need of God, you will not seek him and if you do not seek him, you will not find him.

'Suffering makes us realise that our happiness lies in another world.

'We are like blocks of stone out of which the sculptor carves the forms of men. The blows of his chisel, which hurt us so much, are what make us perfect. The suffering in the world is not the failure of God's love for us; it is that love in action.'

25 October

The gospel says very simply that the heart of our mission is summed up in, 'Love the Lord God with all your heart and your neighbour as yourself.' The heart of the mission then is *love* not law. Where there is no mercy, no love and no compassion God cannot be.

Listen again to what he says: 'You must love the Lord your God with all your hearts, with all your soul, and all your mind.' I must make sure there is nothing in my life which is more important than God. God has to be the centre of everything I do. That's a tough call and that's the law of love.

The second law is really two laws in one. We must love our neighbour as ourselves. And that's the key. If we can't respect ourselves then how can we expect others to respect us and how can we have any respect for others ourselves? If we can't love ourselves we can't love others and we certainly can't love God.

26 October

The Pope at the Wailing Wall

He was being watched by a little man from Belfast. Wasn't sure what the Pope was doing, so he asked an American Cardinal. And the American cardinal told him that he was praying for America, for the American people, for the safety of their troops across the world, for victory over Al Qaida, and for those who died in 9/11. The wee man was impressed.

But he then went further along the wall still not satisfied and he asked a man who turned out to be a Rabbi. And he told him the Pope was praying for Jews and for peace between Jews and Arabs and between Israel and Lebanon and for the chosen people.

Then he noticed that there was an Irish bishop standing beside him and he asked him what the Pope was doing at the Wailing Wall. And the Irish bishop said, 'Well of course the Pope spends his days praying for Ireland.' How was praying for peace between Protestants and Catholics, between Unionists and Nationalists. And most of all he was praying that the Paisleyites and the Sinn Féiners would get together and work for peace.

And the wee man turned away and said, 'No wonder the poor man's talking to the wall.'

27 October

Jesus makes a point in the gospel and it is this: 'Anyone who is not against us, is for us.' That's an amazing quote. It's exactly the opposite to what the church thinks and what we usually would think about ourselves. Churches the world over have fought wars thinking that those who are not *for* them must be *against* them. And we are the same. That's the small mindedness that is rejected by Jesus. He turns it around and looks at it positively and says, 'Anyone who is not *against* you is *for* you.' There's a world of difference in that.

For example, many parents wonder about their children not going to Mass. The whole point is this. It would be lovely if everybody went to Mass and it's a central part of Christian community. But just because people don't go to God the same way as us doesn't mean they are against us. In fact Jesus says, look out and if they are not against you, if they are not actively against you, then you can take it for grant it they are for you. That's the distinction between a miserly religion and an open one like Jesus wants us to have.

We are to see good – not bad – in others. And the same with ourselves. Sometimes we see the worst enemy that is within ourselves. Try looking for what is best.

28 October

There's a lovely story about a Dublin man who took on a job driving a lorry. He had a big load to deliver down to Kerry one day. Whilst he was going through Killarney he saw a notice 'Low Bridge Detour'. But the Dub thought he could get through anywhere in Kerry. He got to the low bridge and was going through nice and slowly and the next thing, crunch! there he was stuck in the middle of the bridge. He couldn't go backwards or forward and didn't know what to do. Most of us would panic, but not the Dub.

He took out a packet of cigarettes and lit one and was smoking away wondering what he should be doing and a Kerry Garda came up and knocked the window. 'Are we stuck?' said the Garda. 'Ah no, I'm just having a wee smoke,' said the Dub. 'Well what are we doing out in the middle of the road then?' says the Garda. 'What have you got in your lorry?' "Ah, don't worry! I'm delivering bridges,' says the Dub.

29 October

Sometimes, as the song says, 'God's greatest gifts to us are unanswered prayers.'

We are to keep on praying, but we must remember that the purpose of our prayer is *not* to change God, but to change us. That's a wonderful insight that we might well spend time listening to.

30 October

I heard a nice little story about a man from East Belfast who came from a puritan background and wasn't allowed to back horses, but he had this urge to do so. So he went down to the Curragh in Kildare and thought he'd be unknown down there. In the first two races he had nearly lost his shirt. He kept a few euros to get him home and he went out the back of the stand to calm himself down. There he saw the horses parading for third race and he noticed that there was a priest who went in, looked at them all and then went over gently to one of them and made what looked like the sign of the cross on the horse's forehead. He looked at the number of the horse but saw that it was a 50-1 chance. So he wouldn't back it. He had lost enough already. But lo and behold didn't the horse win by about five lengths.

For the next race he watched what the priest did and this time it was a 30-1 horse he crossed, so he put a few euro on it and luckily it won. The same happened in the fifth and sixth races. By now he had accumulated a couple of hundred euro. Before the last race he went to the ring to observe the priest again. Not only did he mark his forehead but he put a cross on his ears, his eyes, his nostrils and even on his hooves. He put on every cent he had in his pockets. The horse ran about one hundred yards and then, puffed out, the horse walked back to the start again. He had lost everything. Very annoyed, he went to the priest and asked him why he had let him down. And the priest said to him, 'That's the difficulty with you people from East Belfast. You don't know the difference between a blessing and the last rites.'

31 October

Halloween is a strange day and a time when all of us dabble, perhaps unwittingly, in pagan customs. But don't be too worried. Christians have a habit of making festivals their own.

Halloween has Celtic origins. The name itself now has its origins in the Catholic Church. It's a contraction of All Hallows' Eve. 1 November, All Saints' or All Hallows' Day when all the forgotten saints and hallowed/holy people are remembered, and this is the eve of the feast – Halloween.

My advice is to enjoy the day and don't think too much about where it all came from. Take time as a family to have fun together and find little tricks to give yourself a treat. And anyway, all that fruit and pudding and dressing up will brighten up those dull November nights and help us get through those depressing dark days. Enjoy it while you can. Happy Halloween.

1 November

I was reading a poem of T. S. Eliot recently and a phrase jumped out at me. It said, 'Home is where we start from.'

It set me thinking about the journeys of life. I've got to that age. The earlier part of life can be consumed with untamed rushing at life. My own was filled with impatience to get things done, a longing to achieve something. But I discovered at some point that life had passed me by. I realised I was so far down the road of life that the journey home stared me in the face. That was a mid-life crisis. I got some peace when I settled myself and recognised that I would love to be young again, but I wouldn't want all the turbulence of youth a second time. But the second half of life, I've discovered, demands a journey too. I still need many of the things I've always needed – a sense of identity, a meaning, a purpose in life, a sense of self worth. I also need a sense of intimacy and rootedness. Perfection like peace, comes dropping slow. Physically, spiritually and emotionally I'm reasonably content with where I am at and don't need to be 'on the road' all the time.

That's why the words from T. S. Eliot meant so much to me. 'Home is where we start from.'

2 November

I was reading from the Book of Job in Morning Prayer recently and I was struck by something that I've read for over 40 years without noticing its importance. It said, 'Naked I came from my mother's womb and naked I'll go back.'

That gave me a clue. Peace in the second half of life is about letting go. Mostly we let go of all the things we tried so hard to attain in the first half of life.

But as I think about it now, the things we need to let go most of all are our hurts, fears and wounds. I find most peace when I learn to forgive – others, God and myself. It's impossible to go through life without being wounded. We can't have everything we dreamed of. There's disappointment and anger within us and unless I learn to forgive, I'll give way to bitterness.

3 November

In these islands alone there are now 12 million pensioners. In the developing world there are around 600 million people aged 60 and over. By 2050 there will be 2 billion older people in the developing world. Yet despite that fact, older people often remain the invisible majority. That's why we should celebrate older people at home especially.

In many countries the older generation is left with the burdens of supporting family life. Because of AIDS and other illnesses, millions of children only have grandparents left to care and provide for them. In sub-Saharan Africa 6 million children are looked after by their grandparents.

As the winter really takes hold, this is a good time to look after older people in your home and in your neighbourhood. As we prepare to waste a fortune on useless Christmas presents, would it not be a good idea to set a little money aside to help the old, the poor and the dying? Begin in your local area, but send something to the poor abroad too, for we are all God's children!

4 November

Courage and Conscience
Courage is an inner resolution to go forward despite obstacles;
    Cowardice is submissive surrender to circumstances.
Courage breeds creative self-affirmation;
    Cowardice produces destructive self-abnegation.
Courage faces fear and masters it;
    Cowardice represses fear and is mastered by it.
Cowardice asks the question, is it safe?
    Expediency asks the question, is it politic?
Vanity asks the question, is it popular?
    But conscience asks the question, is it right?
And there comes a time when one must take a position that is neither safe, nor politic, nor popular, but one must take it because it is right.
(From the writings of Martin Luther King Jr)

5 November

When Charlie Roberts murdered five young Amish girls in their one-roomed schoolhouse, the eyes of the world turned on these obscure, gentle and principled people. It's fascinating to discover how a group of people can be so cut off from modern living.

In short they live in a time machine and yet the greatest lesson they have taught us since the murder of their five children is their great ability to forgive. Charlie Roberts, the man who killed their children, was himself a married man with three young children. The Amish community insisted on establishing a fund for his family after he killed himself. They set it up within days of the massacre. Many of the parents of the children who were murdered personally approached Marie Roberts, his wife, to offer their forgiveness to her. And when Roberts was being buried, many of the Amish families asked if it would be possible for them to attend his funeral. Their reason? 'It's very important that we teach the children not to think evil of the man who did this,' they told disbelieving journalists. Their customs may be outdated, but we can still be reminded of some decent principles we have long forsaken.

6 November

When P. W. Botha, the cruellest and most notorious President of South Africa died, many people were surprised, shocked even, at Nelson Mandela's moving message of sympathy to his family. Not only that but he put on record his recognition of the contribution Botha made to peace in that troubled country.

Most people would agree that F. W. De Klerk was the white president who did the most to dismantle the evil of apartheid, but Mandela always believed that if Botha had not taken the first step, then no other steps could have been taken. And that was why he paid a tribute to him on his death.

It's a measure of the man Mandela is that he could do business with such a vicious tyrant and see good in him when most of the world saw only his cruelty. It's a lesson for us all in Ireland. Peace can only be permanent when the most bigoted agree to respect each other and make peace work.

7 November

A most revealing letter: 'Two years ago a new priest arrived at my church. As a devout Catholic I was astounded to be told he was a married priest with twin girls. But once we met him and listened to his sermons and beautiful Mass, we changed completely. We just love him. It's amazing how all the people, especially the old, have accepted him. It's great.' (Susan, Northampton)

Married priests in the Catholic Church works just fine!

8 November

Beatitudes of an Old Person

Happy are they who look at me with kindness.

Happy are they who understand my weary step.

Happy are they who speak loudly to minimise my deafness.

Happy are they who clasp with warmth my shaking hands.

Happy are they who take an interest in my faraway youth.

Happy are they who don't get tired of listening to my stories already too many times repeated.

Happy are they who understand my need for affection.

Happy are they who give me fragments of their time.

Happy are they who remember my loneliness.

Happy are they who draw near to me in my suffering.

Happy are they who give me happiness in this last stage of my life.

Happy are they who are near to me in the moment of my meeting with the Lord.

When I enter the life without end, I will remember them in front of the Lord Jesus.

9 November

During these days in November, many people allow themselves to confront their grief. It's a dark month, full of depression and has the smell of death about it.

When we struggle with death, before long we discover a very simple fact. Ideal deaths happen only in Hollywood. For the rest of us, people die when they have to. They don't wait for the perfect time so that we'll be able to cope. Death happens and we have to make the best of it.

There is such a thing as good grief. And whether we like it or not bereavement is a fact of life. The only way to avoid grief is to avoid love at all cost.

There is no perfect way to grieve. My pain is my own. Your pain is your own. Each of us has to grieve in our own way.

10 November

I became aware of just how invasive CCTV has become because I have been at airports recently. There was a time when I actually enjoyed flying. I hate it now.

To begin with I dread the journey to Dublin airport. By the time I have my car parked I want to go home and by the time I have checked in I promise myself that I will never ever leave dear old Fermanagh again.

There was a time when people who went to an airport were treated as customers; now each of us is man-handled, insulted, searched, photographed, made to take off shoes and belts, have the contents of our bag strewn across a very public desk, and obviously treated as a potential criminal. Regular flyers will go straight to heaven because their purgatory will be done a thousand times over.

11 November

Charles Plumb was a US Navy Pilot in Vietnam who was brave and effective. He had 75 successful missions during the Vietnam War but on his 75th a ground-to-air missile destroyed his plane. He was able to bail out and parachute to the ground. Unfortunately for him, he parachuted into enemy territory, was arrested and spent 6 years in a Vietnamese jail.

One day in a cafe long after the Vietnam War, he was having a cup of coffee with his wife and a man approached Plumb and asked him if he was the Captain Charles Plumb who flew off *Kitty Hawk*. The man then explained that he was one of the sailors on the US navy ship from which Plumb took off.

He explained that his job was to fold and pack the parachutes. 'I must have done a good job because you are still alive,' the man said as he went off into the crowded street. Plumb agreed.

Later that evening, Plumb began to think of how dismissive he had been of this man's work all those years ago. He remembered him at the table and remembered that he often walked past him without even saying hello. He didn't appreciate that his life depended on that man's good work. He had never even thanked him for it. Now Plumb ends his lectures with one simple question: 'Who packs your parachute?'

12 November

I learned a crucial lesson about forgiveness from Gordon Wilson. One day in a peaceful conversation I asked him if he ever regretted his message of forgiveness on the night of Marie's murder. This is what he confided to me. He said that every night before sleeping he prayed to God to be able to forgive her killers again in the morning. Forgiveness was not a once-off decision but an ongoing daily decision that depended on God's grace and his acceptance of that grace. It was worth knowing Gordon for that insight alone.

13 November

I was in London recently and, glancing through various tourists books, I extracted this list of facts which fascinated me. I hope they do you too:

- The new Wembley Stadium has 2618 toilets – more than any other building in the world.
- There are 147 registered parks and gardens in London.
- Londoners produce 3.5m tonnes of rubbish a year.
- The Thames is now clean enough to be a salmon river after a 200 year absence.
- The British Library contains more than 30 million books.
- 200,000 new books are published every year in the UK.
- The great bell in Big Ben weighs 13 tonnes.
- The House of Commons is not big enough to accommodate all its 646 MPs, and seats only two thirds of them at any one time. Late comers are forced to stand at the entrance.
- More people in London now go to a Mosque on a Friday than to a church on Sunday.
- The average overseas business visitor spends £154.00 a day whilst in London. The average tourist spends less than half of that.
- Heathrow handles 68m passengers a year which makes it the world's busiest airport.
- Oxford Street is Europe's longest high street with 200 million shoppers spending £6 billion every year. There are 30,000 shops in London.

14 November

'I bear no ill-will. I bear no grudge. Dirty sort of talk is not going to bring her back to life.' Those words changed Gordon Wilson from a God-fearing Methodist shopkeeper in Enniskillen into an international hero for the cause of peace. They were not cheap words because they cost him dearly, especially within his own community, something I know pained him deeply.

When he gave the interview to BBC Radio Ulster, he had no intention of becoming a hero, or becoming a worldwide voice for peace. He was what he was – a sincere Christian, a grieving father, and a decent man talking.

15 November

I'm special. In all the world there is nobody like me.
Since the beginning of time, there has never been
another person like me.

Nobody has my smile. Nobody has my eyes,
my nose, my hands, my voice. I'm special.

I am the only one in all of creation
who has my set of abilities ...
Through all of eternity no one will ever look,
talk, walk or think like me.

I'm special, I'm rare. And in all rarity there is a great rare value.
Because of my great rare value, I need not attempt to imitate
others. I will accept – yes, celebrate – my differences.

Yes, I'm special.
I am beginning to see that God made me special
for a very special purpose.

God must have a job for me that no one else can do as I.
Out of all the billions of applicants, only one is qualified, only one
has the right combination of what it takes. That one is me.
Because I'm special.

(Anonymous)

16 November

Don't let the sun go down on your anger.

Always set up a time and a place for confrontation. It is important not to blow off steam without thinking. But it is equally important to make a time and place to talk. Don't let it seethe beneath the surface. Face up to it.

The time and place should be reasonably suitable for both parties. Big problems early in the morning are not advisable. A suitable time is important. It should be a quiet place. No TV. No distractions. No in-laws. No children.

17 November

Know what the fight is about.

Many angry people don't know what they are angry about. The issue they think is important isn't the real one, but it's the only one which is manageable right now.

The real issue is suppressed and a little too sensitive to bring to the surface.

Ask yourself: What's really bugging me in this situation? Am I over-reacting? Is it worth all the hassle? If you can put your finger on the trouble state it clearly. Don't conceal it in a mist of words and feelings.

18 November

State your own case. Don't accuse.

In stating your case use 'I-statements'. Don't accuse the other person. If you don't make 'I-statements' you end up calling each other names, e.g. 'You're always worrying,' 'You never talk to me.'

Saying what happens with 'I-statements' makes us deal with facts. It's the difference between venting your anger on the other person and reporting your true feelings. Telling the busy person that they never talk to you is not helpful. Saying that perhaps they should work less and make time for you is more helpful.

19 November

Listen.

A lot more difficult than it seems. It means sitting on the edge of your seat trying to discover what the other person is really saying, even more than concentrating on what to say next, or on being right.

To make sure you've got it right, you should now and then summarise what you think the other person is saying.

Body language is the best clue to whether you're listening or not. Eyes that fidget, glazed look, writing, reading, sneaking a look at television, give the game away.

20 November

Laugh. Particularly at yourself.

I have to deal frequently with self-righteous and pompous people. They're a pain and pathetic.

I long for someone who can have a good laugh. A word of warning though – forget about sarcastic humour at the other's expense. That's viciousness, not humour.

21 November

Be calm.

It's difficult to be calm when someone is being loud-mouthed, unfair, or insists on going for the jugular while you're doing your best to be calm and gentle. Cut your losses with that person. You're not going to get anywhere. Staying calm though in normal circumstances is essential. It doesn't help if you reduce yourself to the level of the other's incompetence.

22 November

Make an agreement.

The make-up kiss, the hug, the smile, the flowers, the night out, the hand shake, are all ways of saying, 'No hard feelings. Let's try again.'

23 November

The F-ing solution.

This means Forgive, Forget, and be Friends. It's hard to forgive. Saying 'I forgive' means the willingness to forgive.

If you find yourself full of anger, that's not failure. It means that you have to turn things over to a Higher Power once again.

Forgetting is wiping the slate clean and not brooding.

Being friends is trying to forge a peaceful climate. It's being as pleasant as you can. 'Be compassionate as your Father is compassionate. Do not judge and you will not be judged. Do not condemn and you will not be condemned. Pardon and you will be pardoned. (Luke 6:36). That's the gospel truth.

24 November

Everyone has known people who kept every law and every com-mandment, but were spiteful, bitter, small-minded, bigoted bullies. There is no holiness where such attitudes thrive. The spiritual life will be blessed with a good spirit, the 'other' life deals with the bad spirits. I don't want to call it evil, but at the moment I can think of no other word for the destruction these 'holy' tyrants cause. There is nothing so detrimental to genuine holiness as a person who keeps all the rules but whose 'god' spreads unhappiness.

I am always reminded of the elder son in the story of the prodigal son. You couldn't fault him for duty, but he wasn't able to celebrate and made himself a sad rejected figure. Holy people should be merciful to themselves and others. They spread peace, understanding and compassion.

25 November

A spiritual journey needs to have an ability to accept difference. I don't have to be perfect myself and I shouldn't expect others to be perfect. I need to seek and be friends with those who are different. Jesus said that we should leave the 99 to look after themselves and go after the one who is lost. I need to respect myself when I am lost and I have to help others when they are lost. Those who are lost are also on a journey.

Grace builds on nature so I need to make sure I am healthy and happy within myself. I have to tackle whatever is humanly dysfunc-tional. If I do that, God's grace will do the rest.

26 November

I want to share a few rules that I use in determining my own spiritual journey. Because I am a Christian, they will focus on Christian spirituality. To me there are a number of essential principles I have to get right in my life if I'm to be honest before God.

The first one is that I have to have personal integrity. I must be able to look at myself in the mirror and be honest. I have to know that I'm not a sham.

Secondly, if I am to be serious about having a Christian spiritual journey, it is absolutely essential that I do everything I can to help the poor. The poor at home, the poor in the Third World, the spiritually poor as well as the materially poor.

Third, I must have community somewhere in my life. There can be no Communion unless I have community. And if there is no communion there's no Eucharist and if there is no Eucharist there is no Christianity.

Fourthly, it is most important that a person who is genuinely trying to be holy, should have a peacefulness and quietness about them. They should be easy to live with.

27 November

Think of the different energy you could have if you promised you would never criticise yourself again. When you accept yourself as you are, you become more forgiving of other people's weaknesses or seeming limitations. You might find people hugging you for no reason!

When we enjoy being ourselves, we find it easier to forgive others for not being perfect. The willingness to forgive comes from our own decision to move beyond self-criticism. Love changes everything.

28 November

There's a useful principle about religion which says: 'God doesn't expect us to take the Bible literally, but he does expect us to take it seriously.'

A man who lived that principle to the full was the Rev Chad Varah. His father was an Anglican Minister and the young Chad, who was called after the patron saint of the parish he was born in, was a bright young man who studied science at university. But at the end of his university training he decided to be like his father and become an Anglican Minister. In 1953 he founded the Samaritans, 'To befriend the suicidal and despairing'. He was inundated with requests and asked fellow clergy for help. He got little. He decided to train the laity to do it. Two great movements were born. One to help the suicidal and one to involve the laity. His basic principle was that we must listen … listen … listen … He knew that ordinary people could do extraordinary things. At the end of his life there were 202 Samaritans Centres in Britain and Ireland with 15,500 volunteers. The Samaritans have spread to 40 countries throughout the world.

At the same time, he was also a science writer who scripted comics like *The Eagle*. He is the man who invented the cartoon Dan Dare.

Chad Varah was one man who took the Bible seriously.

29 November

Albert Einstein once said, 'Only a life lived for others is worth living.' The same thought is put more blandly in an anonymous piece of doggerel: 'I sought my soul but my soul I could not see; I sought my God but God eluded me; I sought my brother and I found all three.'

That rule of life is best summed up in a prayer by John Wesley, one of the founding brothers of the Methodist Movement, who said: 'Do all the good you can, by all the means you can, in all the ways you can, in all the times you can, at all the times you can, to all the people you can, as long as ever you can.'

30 November

A decent woman wrote to me: 'What ever happened to the hope for change many of us had post Vatican II? The wonderful documents compiled by the Council Fathers appear to have been confined to the scrap heap and sometimes it appears as if the Council had never taken place. The idea of the church as the People of God, empowered as they are by their baptism, sharing in the priesthood, prophecy and kingship of Christ as envisaged by *Lumen Gentium* (chap 2) has been ignored by the hierarchical church. The church is today, as it was then, comprised of the passive, paying and praying masses whose insights and talents count for nought.' If only we had a bishop or a clerical leader with this woman's insight.

1 December

I followed with interest the debate in the House of Lords on the Bill For Assisted Dying For The Terminally Ill. Some excellent points were made about what they euphemistically call Assisted Suicide.

In my view killings by the medical profession must always be wrong. But I am equally certain that there is no obligation to go to extreme lengths to prolong life or suffering.

Our duty should be to ease suffering in every possible way. This does not include either deliberately killing off a person whom someone judges to be useless, or helping a person to take their own life.

Many ill patients want to die because 'They don't want to be a burden.' The introduction of assisted suicide would allow a small proportion to commit suicide if they wanted to, but it would also put pressure on others to choose that route, even when they didn't want to. It would relieve their family from burdensome care.

The main conclusion from The Lords' debate was that more money and more resources should be put into palliative care so that a respectful death can be guaranteed to the vast majority of terminally ill patients.

2 December

The Special Child
The child, yet unborn, spoke with the Father,
'Lord, how will I survive in the world?
I will not be like other children. My
walk may be slower, my speech hard
to understand. I may look different.
What is to become of me?'
The Lord replied to the child,
'My precious one, have no fear, I will
give you exceptional parents; they
will love you because you are special,
not in spite of it. Though your path
through life will be difficult, your
reward will be greater, you will have been blessed
with a special ability to love,
and those whose lives you touch will be blessed
because you are special.' *(Author unknown)*

3 December

It's amazing the number people I speak to these days who are disillusioned with the church as an institution. Eventually we always come to the same conclusion. Institutions look after themselves. Almost all of them fail eventually.

So take a look at the institutions you have been giving too much of your life to. Ask yourself a few basic questions like these:

a) What does this institution do for me?

b) What does it do for any human being?

c) If I ceased to be of use to them how would the institution treat me?

d) If the institution collapsed, what would it do to my life?

e) What can I do to change the institution to make it more responsive to this modern world?

Your answers may surprise you!

4 December

If somebody should speak to you about their intention of committing suicide, always take it seriously. Thank them for confiding in you, explain that they are brave people to talk to you so openly. Then ask the question: When did you begin to feel this way? That may give them the confidence to talk things through with you.

The main point is not to ignore it. It's not a help to tell them that their thinking doesn't make sense. You may think it doesn't make sense. But to them it does. We have to accept that. Suicidal people may be incapable of thinking in the normal ways we do. If they did then they wouldn't think of suicide.

Try to get them to seek immediate help. The Samaritans are always available and do excellent work in rescuing people from the verge of the abyss.

5 December

A Russian couple were walking down the street in Moscow one night when the man felt a drop hit his nose.
'I think it's raining,' he said to his wife.
'No, that felt more like snow to me,' she replied.
'I'm sure it was just rain,' he said.
Just then they saw a Communist Party official walking toward them.
'Let's not fight about it,' the man said. 'Let's ask Comrade Rudolph whether it's officially raining or snowing.'
As the official approached, the man said, 'Tell us, Comrade Rudolph, is it officially raining or snowing?'
'It's raining, of course,' he replied, and walked on.
But the woman insisted: 'I know that felt like snow!'
The man quietly replied: 'Rudolph the Red knows rain, dear.'

6 December

I don't mind admitting it – I shed a few tears when I heard that George Best died. Memories – all sorts of them – came flooding back.

In a moment of self analysis, George Best said about himself: 'I was born with a great gift and sometimes with that comes a destructive streak. Just as I wanted to outdo everyone when I played, I had to outdo everyone when we were out on the town ...it all went wrong with football, the thing I loved most of all, and from there my life slowly fell apart.' Sad isn't it. All our worlds eventually fall apart, and what's left then?

Maybe that's what Michael Parkinson meant when he said: 'The only tragedy George Best has to confront is that he will never know how good he could have been.'

Another old friend, Pat Jennings, began his international career with Northern Ireland on the same night as George Best in 1964, when both were raw teenagers. He recalled that he was 'the same George from that first night, right to the very end. There were no airs and graces about him ... George was a lovely man.' And when all is said and done, maybe that's the best way of all to remember a true genius who fought many battles and won only some of them. But thanks for the memories anyway, George.

7 December

This wisdom comes from a *Dear Abbey* letter:

'Dear Readers. Today, take a few minutes to think what you have to be thankful for.

'How's your health? Well, thank God you have lived this long. A lot of people haven't.

'You're hurting? Thousands, maybe millions, are hurting much more. Just visit a hospital or a rehabilitation clinic and see for yourself.

'If you awakened this morning and were able to hear the birds sing and use your vocal chords to utter human sounds and walk to the breakfast table on two good legs, and read the newspaper with two good eyes, praise the Lord, a lot of people couldn't.

'How's your pocket book? Thin? Well, most of the living world is a lot poorer. In fact, one third of the people in the world will go to bed hungry today.

'Are you lonely? If nobody calls you, call them. Go out of your way to do something nice for somebody.

'Are you concerned about your country's future? Good. Our system has been saved by such concern. Concern for honesty in government, concern for peace, and concern for fair play under the law. Your country may not be a rose garden, but neither is it a patch weeds.'

8 December

We are fools whether we dance or not, so we might as well just dance.'

(Japanese proverb)

9 December

'Happy Christmas' we say. But what is happiness? Here area few points to real happiness:

1. First of all leave the past behind.

We all burn energy making martyrs of ourselves. Worse still are the 'if only' brigade. It's as simple as this. What has happened can't be undone. So don't make things worse by throwing a good life after a bad one.

2. Don't make the same mistakes over and over again.

If something goes wrong think about it, spot where it went wrong, then take some action to ensure it doesn't go wrong next time. If you have made a mess of things and said something stupid to another person, don't let it simmer. Say sorry, admit your mistake, it won't kill you.

3. Stop putting yourself down.

Demeaning yourself is not a virtue. Being modest is perfectly acceptable. Being a groveller isn't. If somebody gives you a compliment say thanks and mark it off as a success.

4. Stop worrying about what others think of you.

If you make a mistake it proves one thing. You are part of the human race. But if you paralyse yourself by wondering what other people think, you could be surprised to discover they don't think about you at all. It's your life – make your own decisions.

5. Take charge of your life.

No-one will make things happen for you. You have to make things happen for yourself. And no matter what bad things happen to you in life, do your best to turn it around.

6. Knock down your ivory tower.

More and more people afraid of getting hurt build a tower around themselves. They trust no one. If you keep people out, they will never hurt you, but you'll never live positively either.

7. Be grateful. Those who are grateful for their gifts are always more positive than those who spend their lives complaining about gifts they don't have.

8. Like yourself. It seems obvious when you say it. If you don't like yourself why should anybody else like you? There will be things about yourself that you don't like. Then change them. Don't use them as an excuse to hate yourself.

10 December

Isn't it fantastic the length people will go to ban Christmas? But they won't ban the spending spree. Typical, isn't it, take God out of everything but let nothing disturb the God of commercialism.

I am delighted the Christian Muslim Forum in Britain is pleading with Councils not to suppress Christmas because they say it brings a backlash against Muslims and other non-Christian faiths. They made the valid and common sense point that celebrating Christmas causes little or no offence to minority faiths, but banning offends almost everybody. They added, 'There seems to be a secularising agenda which fails to understands the concerns of religious communities.' The approach is to exclude the mention of any specific religious event or celebration in order to avoid offending anyone. The usual result of such a policy is that it ends up offending most of the population.

11 December

Coming up to Christmas is always a dangerous time for people who feel lonely. There is always a danger they might harm themselves at Christmas simply because emotions run so high. Suicide is a huge problem throughout Ireland.

Many people find that the parts of their lives they are able to cope with throughout the year, become completely overbearing during the Christmas season. They can't find their place in the world, which in turn leads to thoughts of suicide.

If you had a death during the year, you'll understand how out of tune you are with the Christmas spirit. If you had severe depression, how much more trying the Christmas celebrations become. When you feel depressed this spirit of joy and celebration all around is alienating.

It's important to be aware of the danger of suicide. It can help you should those thoughts come your way. It can also help you spot the tell-tale signs in others.

12 December

The Christmas/New Year Holiday is fast becoming a marathon booze-up. Over the Christmas period the average Irish adult consumes 16 litres of alcohol. When you consider the number of non-drinkers there are in the country some of those who drink must consume an average of 5 litres each per day.

To add to this senselessness, we generate so much waste paper that it will be the equivalent weight of 4,000 elephants.

Dustbins will hold:
* fifty four million aluminium beer cans.
* fifteen million beer bottles.
* twenty million wine bottles.
* 2.6 million spirit bottles.
* four million plastic soft drinks bottles.
* twenty-eight million aluminium soft drink cans.
* four million cardboard chocolate boxes.
* three million cardboard toy boxes.
* four million sheets of wrapping paper.

And all this is our way of commemorating a baby who was born to an unmarried mother, in an outhouse with a couple of lowlife shepherds protecting him and a few animals keeping him warm.

Don't worry if you can't make the connection. There is none.

13 December

Some years ago *Dear Abby* had this as a message for the holiday season. She said:

'Dear Readers, we have more to be thankful for than we think. At this time of year take time to think about what we should be more grateful for.

Heavenly Father, we thank you for food – and remember the hungry;
We thank you for health – and remember the sick;
We thank you for friends – and remember the friendless;
We thank you for freedom – and remember the enslaved.'

14 December

Christmas in Heaven
I see the countless Christmas trees around the world below.
With tiny lights like heaven's stars reflecting the snow.
The sight is so spectacular please wipe away the tear
For I'm spending Christmas with Jesus this year.

I hear the many Christmas songs that people hold so dear
But the sounds of music can't compare with the Christmas choir up here.
I have no words to tell you the joys their voices bring
For it's beyond description to hear the angels sing.

I know how much you miss me; I see the pain inside your heart
But I am not so far away, we really aren't apart.
So be happy for me, dear ones, you know I hold you dear
And be glad I'm spending Christmas with Jesus Christ this year.

I sent you each a special gift from my heavenly home above,
I sent you each a memory of my undying love.
After all love is a gift more precious than pure gold.
It was always most important in the stories Jesus told.

Please love and keep each other as my Father said to do.
For I can't count the blessing of love he has for each of you.
So have a merry Christmas and wipe away that tear.
Remember I am spending Christmas with Jesus Christ this year.

(This lovely poem was written by a 13-year-old boy named Ben. He died of a brain tumour he had battled with for over four years. He died on 14 December 1997. He gave this poem to his Mum before he died.)

15 December

'Be who you are and say what you feel because those who mind don't matter and those who matter don't mind.'
(Dr Seuss)

16 December

There is a story told about a man who met a beggar in the street one day. He's a shabby looking homeless man and he asks him for money to buy a meal. The man is feeling good that day so he takes out £10 out of his wallet and begins to ask him questions. He says, 'I want to make sure you are not going to spend this money on drink.' The beggar tells him, 'Drink is what put me on the street. I gave it up years ago. I'm never likely to go back on it again.'

'Maybe with that rattly cough you have it's smoking that you spend your money on.' The beggar replied, 'I never smoked in my life. And the rattly cough is from sleeping out in the damp streets for ten years.'

'I hope you wouldn't go and spend it on a horse?' To which the beggar replies, 'Gambling is a mug's game. I don't have a penny to gather enough food, so I'm not likely to waste it on a horse I don't even know.'

'Well there's a red-light district just around the corner, how am I to know you are not going to spend the money there?' The beggar answered, 'Can you not see that a homeless, dirty, smelly old beggar like me wouldn't get anywhere even in a red-light district for a £100, never mind £10?'

The man finally gave in and said, 'Well I'm not going to give you the £10. Instead I'm going to bring you home and I'm going to ask my wife to cook you the best meal you have ever had.'

The homeless man was amazed. 'Won't your wife be furious with you for doing that? I'm dirty and smelly and she won't want me in your house.'

To which the man replied, 'Don't worry about that. I just want my wife to see what happens a man who doesn't drink, smoke, gamble or go with women.'

We can twist facts to suit ourselves. And we need to be careful about that when we are trying to find out what sort of God we adore.

17 December

'The slanderous tongue kills three: the slandered, the slanderer and he who listens to slander.'
(The Talmud)

18 December

Consider the real sights and sounds and tastes – and SMELLS – experienced by the family of Joseph, Mary and the child on that night centuries ago:

- the damp, aching cold of a cave along the Bethlehem hillside
- the burning in the eyes and throat from days of travelling on foot on hard, dusty roads
- the terror of finding yourself homeless, stranded in an unknown town, with no place to stay
- the paralysing fear that robbers and wild animals could strike out of nowhere
- the silence of the night broken only by the cry of wolves and the bleating of sheep
- the anguish of a young woman delivering her first child alone, with her carpenter husband offering what help he can
- the overwhelming stench of a cave used as a barn: the smell of animals, manure, urine and perspiration.

Ironically, the night we celebrate with such magnificent solemnity was actually rather disgusting.

19 December

In Britain a third of schools will not be holding a Carol Service. Traditional Christmas celebrations are shunned in case non-Christians might be upset.

Some brave teachers are speaking out against it. One Head is convinced Christmas has been side-lined in schools. 'Increasingly we are celebrating all other world religions, making sure we are not offending anyone, but then not acknowledging our own – even at Christmas,' he said.

Perhaps one reason is that in a recent poll 33% of teachers in Britain admitted that they don't believe in God. And a quarter of secondary teachers refused to take part in acts of collective worship.

Extraordinarily it comes at a time when governments around the world are saying that minority religions and secular values should be taught. Don't ask me to make sense of the nonsensical.

20 December

If you have been lucky enough to be off the drink for a while, Christmas will be tough. Here are a few tips that might get you through it sober. If you can stay sober it will be a marvellous achievement for yourself, but it will be sheer bliss for those whose Christmases you have destroyed in the past:

- Don't let what others say and do be an excuse for you drinking. No-one but yourself is responsible for your drinking. You make the decisions.
- Avoid self-pity and stop dwelling on the past. If there is something you are angry about, deal with it. Don't let it fester. Otherwise you are only looking for an excuse to drink.
- If you chose to stop drinking or were advised to do it and found it easy, you may catch yourself thinking you could now have the odd drink without any harmful effects. Don't fool yourself.
- You'll think of plenty of reasons for going back on the drink. But remember that drinking controls your life and once you start, it takes over your life.
- Think again about the reasons why you stopped drinking in the first place. List in your mind and, if possible, on paper the bad things about your drinking – and the good things about your being sober.
- Don't be afraid to talk to yourself. Come up with little phrases that make sense. 'One day at a time.' 'I decided not to drink. I have the sense not to drink.'
- Be aware of over confidence and false friends.
- Remember the word H.A.L.T. Don't get too Hungry, too Angry, too Lonely or too Tired! There's a marvellous philosophy of life in that one word.

Above all stay sober and stay safe.

21 December

Amy Jo wrote to Santa and sent her letter to the local radio station: 'I have a problem in school. Kids laugh at me because of the way I walk and talk. I have cerebral palsy. I just want one day where no one laughs at me or makes fun of me.'

When station workers read it, they knew they had to do something. Amy Jo wasn't asking for much – just one day without teasing and bullying. The workers read Amy Jo's letter on the air.

The result? Amy Jo's simple request was reported in newspapers around the world, tugging at people's heartstrings and needling their consciences. Everyone could relate to her pleas for respect, whether they shared her problem or were themselves the cause of the problem.

In her hometown, Amy Jo received her day of goodwill from classmates, and the mayor proclaimed December 21 as Amy Jo Day.

But the best part was learning that teachers and parents from all over the world were using her letter as a springboard to discuss discrimination. Amy Jo's letter to Santa had not only benefited her, but also prevented other children from experiencing the pain she had known.

Before Santa was due to arrive, Amy Jo had already received much more than she'd wished for.

22 December

From Aesop's Fables comes this little reminder about vanity and self-discipline.

A coal-black crow once stole a piece of meat. She flew to the tree and held the meat in her beak.

A fox who saw her wanted the meat for himself, so he looked up the tree and said, 'How beautiful you are, my friend. Your feathers are fairer than the dove's. Is your voice as sweet as your form is beautiful? If so you must be the queen of the birds.'

The crow was so happy in his praise that she opened her mouth to show how she could sing. Down fell the piece of meat.

The fox seized upon it and ran away.

23 December

Christmas waste frightens me. There will be four and a half million presents opened this weekend which will be immediately dumped as unwanted or useless. The total cost will be 200 million euro. All this in the name of a child who had nowhere to lay his head, no house to call his own, and no clothes except the ones he was wrapped in.

There is a good side to all of this. In the face of disaster, nowhere responded more magnificently than Ireland. There's a great well of human decency when people are in need. We recognise that there is only one face to grief, no matter how many languages or skin colours. All human hearts break, all human eyes cry bitter tears and all good people respond heroically and generously.

Instead of wasting those four and half million presents, wouldn't it be a good idea if they were collected, sent to a central depot and sold to help the poor of the world. There aren't many unforgivable sins, but unnecessary waste is definitely one of them.

24 December

If they've heard of him at all, many presume Ben Stein is just a quirky actor/comedian who talks in a monotone. Anyway, he had this to say about doing away with Christmas:

'I am a Jew, and every single one of my ancestors was Jewish. And it does not bother me even a little bit when people call those beautiful lit up, bejewelled trees Christmas trees. I don't feel threatened. I don't feel discriminated against. That's what they are: Christmas trees.

'Doesn't bother me a bit when people say, "Merry Christmas" to me. I don't think they are slighting me or getting ready to put me in a ghetto. In fact, I kind of like it. It shows that we are all brothers and sisters celebrating this happy time of year.

'I don't like getting pushed around for being a Jew, and I don't think Christians like getting pushed around for being Christians. I think people who believe in God are sick and tired of getting pushed around, period.'

25 December

Here are Ten Commandments to help make Christmas more enjoyable for yourself and more rewarding for everyone:

1. I will examine my motives for celebrating Christmas.
2. I will share in the work of preparing for Christmas.
3. I will not spend money to impress others.
4. I will not engage excessively in eating, drinking or partying and will have alternatives to alcohol when I entertain.
5. I will not buy items made by workers whose wages and working conditions are unjust.
6. I will avoid buying gifts made by processes that pollute the environment.
7. I will question the source of consumer goods before I buy.
8. I will celebrate Christmas by sharing more of myself and my property.
9. I will use some of my time to visit family and friends and someone who has been forgotten.
10. I will spend some time in prayer this Christmas.

26 December

I love Christmas stories. The late Cardinal Hume was preaching one Christmas morning in a small parish in North London. To the surprise of many, he didn't mention the birth of our Lord. Instead he told the congregation the true story of what happened in a concentration camp during World War II.

The people had to queue, waiting for their turn to enter the chambers of death. When the doors closed, the cut-off point came as a young Jewish girl was standing alone crying, naked and shivering with fear. The next time the doors opened she would be the first in. She was clutching tightly her only worldly possession, a small rag doll.

Everyone around her was understandably preoccupied with their own worries. No one even noticed her shaking and shivering. No one, that is, except the German guard whose job it was to mercilessly shunt these unfortunate people to their death. The guard was so moved by her crying that he immediately took off his own clothes, took her hand and stood next to her without saying a word.

Instantly the little girl's face lit up. She stopped crying and when the doors of the chamber reopened they both entered together hand in hand.

The Cardinal made the point that this is exactly what Christ did 2000 years ago. He broke into our human situation and as St Paul says, 'He has taken our hands and removed our sinful condition.'

27 December

One day a priest who was pastor of a New York church discovered that, for no apparent reason, an elderly lady in his parish took a vehement dislike to him and made no secret of the fact. She told everyone she met she couldn't abide him. And, as is the case in all small parishes, word eventually reached the pastor himself.

He dreaded the day when parish calls would take him to her door.

And, when the day came, he paced back and forth in front of the building, trying to work up the courage to go in.

He was secretly hoping she would not be home and he was praying he would be able to leave his card and exit discreetly.

So he climbed the stairs and knocked on the door. There was no answer.

He knocked again and heard a sound inside, so he knelt down and looked through the letterbox to see if anyone was there. To his surprise he saw an eye staring back at him.

With a chuckle the woman remarked, 'Father, this is the first time we have seen eye to eye!'

'Yes,' he replied, 'And we had to get down on our knees to do it!'

28 December

From Mother to Child
I gave you life, but cannot live it for you.
I can give you directions, but I cannot force you to follow them.
I can take you to church each Sunday, but I cannot make you believe.
I can give you love, but I cannot make you take it.
I can teach you to share, but I cannot make you unselfish.
I can teach you respect, but I cannot force you to be honourable.
I can advise you about friends, but cannot choose them for you.
I can advise you about sex, but I cannot keep you pure.
I can tell you about alcohol and drugs, but I cannot say 'no' for you.
I can teach you about kindness, but I cannot force you to be courteous.
I can pray for you, but I cannot make you walk with God.
I can tell you how to live, but I cannot give you eternal life.
I can love you with unconditional love all of my life
and I always will.

29 December

Aesop also supplies a simple little story about compassion.

One day a great lion lay asleep in the sunshine. A little mouse ran across his paw and wakened him. The great lion was going to eat him up when the little mouse cried, 'Oh please, let me go, sir. Some day I may help you.'

The lion laughed at the idea that the little mouse could be of any help to him. But he was a good-natured lion, and he set the mouse free.

Not long after, the lion got caught in a net. He tugged and pulled with all his might, but the net was too strong. Then he roared loudly. The little mouse heard him and ran to the spot.

'Be still, dear lion, and I will set you free. I will gnaw the ropes.'

With his sharp little teeth the mouse cut through the net, and the lion came out of the net.

'You laughed at me once,' said the mouse. 'You thought I was too little to do you a good turn. But you see you owe your life to a little mouse.'

Which shows that compassion lies within the power of the mighty and the meek.

30 December

Things you may not know about Christmas

1. The name Christmas comes from the Old English *Cristes Maesse* meaning Mass of Christ.
2. The feast of Christmas is first mentioned in the Roman Chronograph of 354.
3. The date of Christ's birth is not known exactly. Modern scholars suggest around 6 BC.
4. In the East the Nativity was celebrated originally on 6 January.
5. The custom of the Christmas crib was made popular by St Francis of Assisi in 1223.
6. The Christmas tree comes from the Paradise tree which was adorned on 24 December in honour of Adam and Eve.
7. The Christmas tree first appeared in 1605 in Strasbourg.
8. The first Christmas hymns date back to the 5th century.
9. Christmas carols began in Italy and were greatly influenced by St Francis of Assisi.
10. Gifts are given by the French on 1 January, by the Spaniards and Italians on 6 January, not on 25 December.
11. St Nicholas, the patron of children, was the original inspiration behind Santa Claus.

31 December

In Ireland alone unwrapped paper from our presents over the Christmas period is equivalent to the weight of 4,000 elephants. Add to that wine bottles, cans, chocolate boxes and the experts estimate that there will be 130 million containers of rubbish sent to landfill sites in the New Year. What a load of rubbish that is.

Another fact is that the Samaritans, throughout the country, got a call every 7 seconds over the Christmas period. People given to depression and loneliness are at greater danger during the Christmas period when everybody else seems to be enjoying the fun. But if you need to talk at any time during the year, be sure to call the Samaritans where you can talk anonymously and confidentially on 1850 60 90 90 for the price of a local call, 24 hours a day.